# . . . Then The War Came

A Chronology of the Second World War

in Beverley and District

1938 to 1945

by

**Peter H. Robinson**

HUTTON PRESS

1989

Published by the Hutton Press Ltd.
130 Canada Drive, Cherry Burton, Beverley
East Yorkshire HU17 7SB

*Printed and Bound by*

*Clifford Ward & Co. (Bridlington) Ltd.*
*55 West Street, Bridlington, East Yorkshire*
*YO15 3DZ*

ISBN 0 907033 85 7

*DEDICATION*

*"Then the War came" is dedicated to my Mother
who lovingly saw me through so many 'wars'
and always found a Peace.*

## ACKNOWLEDGEMENTS

As I am sure you will realize, no book of this content could have been achieved without a great amount of help and support. This has come in all manner of ways from sharing a memory to loaning a photograph, directing me to the right area or person for help and the loan of personal diaries. To everyone who has contributed in any way no matter how small, I thank them all; but in particular I wish to express my appreciation to the following:

The Beverley Borough Council, Museum of Army Transport, Hilda Robinson, Violet Rose, Katie Oxtoby, Beryl Brown, Philip Robinson of Simsons, Mrs Thelma Symmons, Kathleen Finch, Mrs L. Allison, Doreen Clark, Mrs R. McFarlane, Joan Veitch, Andrew Lock, Andrew Dickinson, Steve Goodhand, Violet Moore, Jessie Oston, Janet Grimes, Neil McRitchie, Lily Penny, Irene Goodyear, Robert Curry, Alastair Newall, Robert Adrian Smales, Grace Martin, Hull Central Library, Alison Morris and the Hull Daily Mail, Mark Wilford and the Beverley Guardian, Paul Downey and the Beverley Advertiser, Moe Smith and the Pocklington Post, the Imperial War Museum, and Her Majesty's Stationery Office.

Peter Harvatt Robinson
Beverley
September 1989

# CONTENTS

BRITISH CURRENCY
CONVERSION CHART

| POUNDS, SHILLINGS AND PENCE | | NEW PENCE |
|---|---|---|
| $\frac{1}{4}$d | Farthing | 0.1p |
| $\frac{1}{2}$d | Ha'penny | 0.21p |
| 1d | Penny | 0.42p |
| 3d | Threepence | 1.25p |
| 6d | Sixpence | 2.5p |
| 1/- | Shilling | 5p |
| 2/- | Florin | 10p |
| 2/6 | Half Crown | 12.5p |
| 5/- | Crown | 25p |
| 10/- | Ten Shillings | 50p |
| £1 | Pound | 100p |
| 1gn | Guinea | 105p |

Britain converted to decimal currency on 15th February 1971.

Steve Oldfield 1988

# INTRODUCTION

Some people have asked why I chose to write about the Second World War. "Why not?" I replied. "Well, how can you possibly know anything about it?" they said.

I graciously acknowledged the compliment adding that I *was* there....well just, and learning to walk, while on the other side of the Channel Hitler's troops marched towards our shores. So that ended that conversation. I decided what I didn't know I would discover for myself through research.

These thoughts were reaffirmed after a 'phone call, followed by a meeting, with a television programme researcher. He wished to access film showing activities in East Yorkshire during the last war for a proposed television series. The aim of the finished programme was to reflect life in wartime Britain.

I welcomed the opportunity to be involved and directed him towards surviving films made by the late Ernest Symmons who had faithfully recorded so many wartime events for his *Playhouse News.* These included footage taken after the severe bombings in Hull, and a subsequent Royal visit. Eventually "A People's War" appeared on our television screens.

Viewing the series fired my enthusiasm even more, and I allowed myself a little pride in knowing that I had indirectly contributed to the making of it.

Initially my researches were centred on Beverley, but I soon realised that although the backbone to the project was Beverley, in so many respects it was really 'Anytown'. And there must have been dozens of places like it throughout the country, with a target city like Hull on their doorstep. These 'Anytowns' accepted the war situation, but were thankfully hardly affected to the extent that the blitzed cities were.

However, the Beverleys of the country did run the full course of the war in every respect with the preparation, personnel training, public information and awareness....the list goes on. Then there was the great influx of military personnel and their effect on the community; we had the RAF close by at Leconfield, and the Army at their barracks on Victoria Road. Effectively the town *was* invaded but didn't suffer; on the contrary many people and businesses benefited from the additional revenue in circulation!

But these were the days of rationing, double summer-time and of course the black-out. These and a great many more aspects of life during the years 1938 to 1945 can be discovered in the pages that follow (athough I feel sure there must be many things I shall have missed).

The presentation of the project concerned me; I pondered deeply on the best way to deliver 'my story'. Of course, how stupid, the obvious had eluded me — it had to be in chronological order.

So, over eighteen months my researches took the form of a diary or catalogue of the war, covering in main the local activity; the relative calm of Beverley running parallel to the drama as it unfolded in Hull, and of course the international situation.

Help and inspiration during the project came from numerous sources; the Museum of Army Transport in Beverley, and Eden Camp at Malton both afforded me that 'feel' for the war. The Channel 4 series "A People's War" proved invaluable, as did the surviving films made by Ernest Symmons and kindly loaned for research by the Beverley Borough Council.

Yet again I found those old "Beverley Guardians" as precious as ever and acknowledge with thanks the Editor of the East Yorkshire Newspaper Group, Mr Jeremy Ashcroft-Hawley, for granting me permission to reproduce items from their newspapers. My thanks also to the Director of Leisure Services for allowing me photographic access to those newspapers under the care of the Beverley Public Library. I must also offer sincere thanks to the staff of the Library's reference section: Pam Martin, Jenny Stanley and Chris Davey, all who gave me immense help over those many months.

As the project developed, I was joined by one of my previous collaborators, Paul Hesp, who I thank here for a considerable amount of initial research.

Steve Oldfield, also involved with previous books, has yet again, afforded me a great deal of help and support in a variety of ways, for which I thank him.

Access to photographic material was at one time a great worry and I felt the project would be minus a good visual record, but thanks to Geoff Oxley and the Hull City Record Office for making available their archive material. The blitzed city of Hull is presented in dramatic detail. However, as photographic records became available help was needed to both research and collate the photographs. Thankfully Andrew Walker, a friend of many years, came to my rescue — his interest in photography proved a valuable asset. Slowly and methodically he sifted through files and photos, the results of which can be seen in the following pages.

Thanks also to Anita Wain for again helping with some of the typing, and to Sharon Austin for her skills on the word processor. And a big Thank You to Charles and Dae Brook of Hutton Press Ltd — they liked the idea and are responsible for bringing my efforts to your bookshelf. I hope you like it too.

Have you got your gas mask? Right, then join me now in 1938 as the country prepares for war.

*"WAR IS A SAVAGE BEAST " by Doreen Morfitt*

*War is a hungry beast,*
*On men it likes to feast,*
*It eats their lives,*
*Leaves sobbing wives,*
*Yes, war is a hungry beast.*

*War is a savage beast,*
*That cares not in the least,*
*If children die,*
*And mothers cry,*
*Yes, war is a savage beast.*

*War is a cruel beast,*
*Cares not for West nor East,*
*Nor men indeed,*
*Whatever creed,*
*Yes, war is a cruel beast.*

*Yet men still fight,*
*To preserve the right,*
*For people to live free.*

*But still –*
*War is a hungry,*
*War is a cruel,*
*War is a savage beast!*

## PRELUDE

April 20th 1989 could have been a date for Adolf Hitler to celebrate, for on that day he would have reached his century, but by his own hand he didn't.

However, in little over four months after Hitler's fiftieth birthday in 1939, he was instrumental in introducing the world to its Second World War.

Hitler had lurked around in the wings for quite some time, and as early as 1925 had made known his anti-semitic views, principally through the publication of his book "Mein Kampf" (My Struggle).

But it wasn't until January 30th 1933 that he made his appearance at the front of the German stage when he was appointed as Chancellor of Germany. Ten months later Germany withdrew from the League of Nations.

On March 16th 1935, Hitler decreed universal Military service for Germany and denounced the Versailles Treaty disarmament clauses.

July 1936 saw the start of the Spanish Civil War, and a year later the bombing of the Spanish town of Guernica.

Here in Britain, the Cinema newsreels presented to the British public the graphic horror of that war — it could have almost been a dress rehearsal and everyone hoped that it would never happen here.

But the reality of an impending war gathered momentum, when in March 1938 Barcelona was on the receiving end of an air attack which left 3,000 casualties.

Soon a new page in the History of Britain would be written, but were its people prepared for what was to come? ....... many tried hard to believe they were.

# 1938

Did you know in 1938 a Murphy Wireless could be rented from Briggs and Powell for 2/3 per week? and if you kept up your payments, within two years you could own the radio; also if you had £168 then it was possible to buy an ex-works 10 H.P. Vauxhall Saloon car from Gordon Armstrongs. Down the street Jebson the butcher was selling English Streaky sliced bacon at 1/2 per pound.

On March 6th birthday greetings were the order of the day for Mrs Emma Frankish of Norwood Dale, when she celebrated her 102nd birthday.

At the end of March, approval was granted for expenditure of £160,000 on extensions and improvements to Leconfield Aerodrome. This was a considerable sum of money, especially as the airfield had only opened sixteen months earlier on December 3rd 1936. But by then the situation in Europe was showing no signs of improving. On the contrary the month of March had seen the annexation of Austria and the Germans entering Prague.

Leconfield aerodrome was situated about 2 miles north of Beverley, within the boundaries of the Hull-Scarborough railway line on the east, and the Beverley to Driffield road on the west. Even so, in these confines the site was chosen for development as a bomber command and provided all the facilities needed for such a base. Its wartime history is interesting and chequered, but that's another story. However, I was interested to discover that a few miles east of Leconfield there was a decoy airfield at Routh — it was listed as a 'Q' site although its purpose is not clear as there is no record of there being any dummy buildings or aircraft.

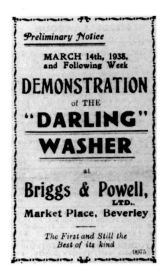

Advertisement for the "Darling Washer" in the Beverley Guardian.

Meanwhile, in other parts of the country the storage and distribution of gas masks had become a problem. In April, the Mayor, Councillor C.H. Burden, appealed for volunteers to help as Air Raid Wardens, should the possibility of war become a reality.

During May, the Air Raids Precautions Sub-Committee recommended that authority be given to the Borough Surveyor to make arrangements to convert the Woodwork Centre in Lord Roberts Road into a respirator store and that Walkergate, St Nicholas and Minster Boys' Schools should, along with the Hall, all be used as respirator distribution centres.

Tuesday June 14th brought the Grand Opening of the new offices and works of Armstrongs Patent Co. Ltd. in Eastgate, but if you were not fortunate enough to attend this event, then you could catch the occasion recorded on celluloid by the Manager of the Playhouse Cinema, Mr Ernest Symmons, for supporting his usual programme for the week commencing June 20th his local newsreel contained film showing the opening of the new premises, as well as "Scenes at the Beverley and East Riding Laundry".

On the night of August 6th/7th 1938, the first 'intended' blackout was operated between the hours of 1.00 and 3.00 a.m. The public were asked to ensure that lights were either extinguished or screened by dark curtains or blinds during that period; also in August, Messrs. Cook, Welton and Gemmell Ltd. (Shipbuilders) were requested to supply steel shutters to protect the engine and filter rooms of the Water Works against possible bomb damage.

On a lighter note, in that year of impending gloom, the Beverley Railway Station was again awarded a First Class prize in the "Brighter Stations" competition, all thanks to the Station Master and his staff who for many months had worked hard to provide an elaborate display of colour, which brought favourable comments from many townsfolk.

It was sad to note that on Monday September 19th, Mrs Emma Frankish of Norwood Dale passed away, although her health had been poor over the previous six months; a fall downstairs may have been partly responsible for her death. Mrs Frankish had celebrated her 102nd birthday in March and two years earlier on her 100th birthday, she received a telegram from His Majesty, King Edward VIII.

During September an unpleasant situation had developed between Czecho-slovakia and Germany over a border principality, which by October had been invaded.

In October, the Gas Mask storage problem had been resolved to a certain extent, and in Beverley on Sunday October 2nd, the first distribution took place. One Adult person from each household was required to attend a centre to collect a gas mask for each person living in the house, and at the same time be instructed on its fitting and use. Some of the masks that had arrived had not been assembled and were in separate parts, but this had posed no problems, especially as Mr Gordon Armstrong had made a generous offer to have them assembled at his Eastgate factory.

It was suggested, and encouraged, by the Corporation that the population dig trenches at the bottom of their gardens for their family's use. "A competent man" was engaged by the Corporation to take charge of the trench digging and was available to give advice to any householders who might encounter problems.

A specimen trench had been made for the public to inspect, situated on a piece of land at the junction of Admiral Walker Road and Lairgate, being 15 feet long, 6 feet 6 inches deep and 3 feet wide. It was hoped that potential trench diggers would dig their own to this format.

It is interesting to note just how well preparations were going on the home front for war. Although the situation in Europe was far from comfortable, the Prime Minister, Neville Chamberlain announced "Peace in our time". However, it would be just over a year before the "phoney war" became a reality.

Two First Aid Stations were established in the Borough and the Public Baths in Ladygate were to be used as a Decontamination Centre.

The Borough Surveyor, Mr John Gouldsmith, had started organizing teams of men for their role in rescue work and demolition of damaged buildings. The Town Clerk, Mr John Dennett, was appointed to the position of Food Executive Officer and the Mayor, Councillor C.H. Burden, was Chairman of the Air Raid Precautions Committee. During the first week in October the Mayor and members of the A.R.P. Committee appealed at the towns three Cinemas for volunteers.

The Postmaster, Mr B.S. Jones, had done everything in his power to ensure that the Government Air Raid Booklet had been delivered to each house in the town before October 1st.

The Booklet gave details on what to do in an Air Raid and guidance on how to make sure that one room in the home could be made gas-proof.

However, amidst the shivers of war preparation, people still believed there would be a tomorrow and at least a Christmas in 1938. Readers of the Beverley Guardian in October were urged by Messrs. Welburn and Glenton, Grocers, to join their Christmas club and at the same time were advised that a "gas-proof device" for babies and young children was in production and would soon be available. In the meantime, protection could be afforded by wrapping a child completely in a blanket and that "it could with safety be carried through gas to the nearest gas-proof shelter".

Still with gas and masks, the next task to be undertaken was the distribution of boxes to store them in, when not in use, as it was important that they be kept in good condition by protecting them from strong light and heat. "Special Air Raid Wardens" would be visiting each house to ensure that everyone had a mask of the correct size and knew how to use it.

An anticipated problem to be considered was that of evacuation from Hull. It was already known that it was possible for over 75,000 people to be sent to Beverley Railway Station, 10,000 of whom would have to be sent on to the country district. The headache was how many places could be made available in the town in a short space of time to take the evacuees?

A total escape from any thoughts of war could be had at the Cinema for 1/-or 1/6 (inc. tax), when the Playhouse presented the first Walt Disney animated feature film "Snow White and the Seven Dwarfs", and as thoughts of Christmas drew ever closer, it was time to think of cakes, puddings and mince-pies. The Rambla Bakery advertised Christmas cakes from 2/6 to 12/6; a one-and-a-half pound Christmas pud was 2/-; and short and puff pastry mince-pies a penny each.

H.W. Brough in Butcher Row offered Gilbey's Spey Royal Whisky at 6/6 and 12/6 a bottle!, while a small bottle of Gilbey's Sherry would set you back 4/-.

And for that last minute special Christmas present for a lady, Heaps and Sons could solve the problem with a platinum set diamond ring at prices from 25/-, and for him a pocket watch at 5/-.

On December 24th 1938, the Beverley Guardian carried on its front page a table showing comparative figures of volunteers plus those still needed for the various services:

| Service | Total Required | In Training | Still Required |
|---|---|---|---|
| Wardens | 180 | 42 | 57 |
| Casualties Service | 120 | 40 | 29 |
| Fire Precautions | 36 | 22 | 13 |
| De-Contamination | 18 | 2 | 8 |
| Rescue & | | | |
| Demolition | 42 | 41 | NIL |
| Clerical | 33 | NIL | 16 |
| Special Services: | | | |
| Gas | 12 | NIL | NIL |
| Water | 5 | NIL | NIL |
| Anti Gas | | | |
| Instructors | 9 | 9 | NIL |

Then followed a list of equipment that would be supplied to the wardens:
"180 civilian duty respirators, 180 armlets, 180 steel helmets, 80 full suits of light anti-gas clothing, 40 large manuscript books, 120 electric torches, 120 whistles, 80 hand rattles, 40 hand bells, 40 small first aid boxes".

Particularly interesting is how the public baths would be used as a decontamination centre. In an emergency an entrance would be provided from the passage at the rear of the baths (an emergency entrance already existed through the boiler house), and the "clean" entrance for those going on and off duty would be through the double doors in Ladygate. An undressing room would be provided at the rear of the boiler house, four showers fixed in the dressing booths and the windows covered with wooden shutters.

Christmas 1938 was one of those rare white ones, snow having fallen almost a week before the festive day and lasting for a few days after; Beverley that year presented a real Christmas card scene.

And so 1938 ended on a peaceful note, the townsfolk were aware of the future and what it held, but at least preparations had been made and the public prepared for a possible gas attack.

Memories of the last Christmas before war was declared are charmingly told by Joan Veitch who was just entering her teenage years. Joan's account of that time is presented vividly here in her own words.

"Christmas 1938 had been the usual jolly affair at my grandparents, with the whole tribe of relatives present. But at midnight in the hall as farewells were made beside the huge old grandfather clock decorated with silver balls and mistletoe, with everyone wishing Happy New Year, I suddenly spoke words that came unbidden to my mind. "Let's hope there isn't a war before next Christmas." For an instance there was a shocked silence, then an uncle glossed over my words, "Yes, let's wish everybody a happy, peaceful New Year," and the friendly chatter of farewells continued."

# 1939

With the New Year two weeks old, the famous "Green's Almanac" came on sale, 1939 making it the eighty-fourth year of publication, and good value at only 2d.

On Saturday January 14th at noon, the newly fitted Air Raid Siren on the Sessions House was tested and at 11 a.m. on the Monday following the whole town's system of sirens was sounded.

If Christmas hadn't left you too short of cash, then a visit to Reynolds' sale at Railway Street corner could yield you a few bargains. They offered 10 windows of them: pure full size sheets (hemmed) 6/11 quality at only 5/- per pair, pure wool blankets full size 25/11 quality at 19/11 a pair, and for the man who wanted that "tunic shirt", there were oddments priced at 3/11, 4/11, 5/11, all reduced to clear at 2/11.

A splash of colour during the dark winter came in the way of "Technicolor" with the film presentation at the Playhouse Cinema of Anna Neagle in "Sixty Glorious Years". The publicity boasted that it had been 'Filmed throughout in Technicolor'.

But no matter what the distraction, there was still unrest in the air, that war could be just around the corner; in fact during February, advice for dog owners was available free from the Canine Defence League on how to fire proof wooden constructions used to house dogs, offering protection from incendiary bombs. However thoughts of summer were around with an announcement in the Beverley Guardian that an Assistant Baths Attendant was to be appointed for the Summer season at a weekly wage of £2-7-0, but summer was still a long way off.

The same newspaper announced that January 1939 had been a record month for recruitment to the Territorial Army. Returns had shown that 4,492 had joined bringing their strength up to 205,267 and during that same month the Auxilliary Territorial Service was strengthened, with 1,764 women joining.

For those not in uniforms, then Montague Burtons could offer a 4 guinea value suit for just 45/-, made to measure, and should the man about town wish to go to town, then 32/7 would buy a monthly return ticket to London.

Although the actual reality of war was still some months away, preparations were well in hand. By February 1939 extensive training had begun for Beverley's Air Raid wardens on the action to be taken for the evacuation of children if the worst happened.

The Market Place became the centre of attraction on a chilly night in late February, for a demonstration of public air raid precautions. This was noted as being the first such event in the country. 150 Special Constables, the Borough Fire Brigade, along with 37 members from the Auxilliary Fire Service and soldiers from the 5th Battalion of the Green Howards, were all there for a demonstration and exercise in dealing with gas decontamination and the dangers of incendiary bombs.

A stall displayed both civilian and service respirators with examples from the first war, plus a good supply of application forms for potential volunteers.

At 8 p.m. the key siren on the Sessions House sounded; this heralded the sounding of other sirens placed in strategic places throughout the town — as far apart as the shipyard at the east end of Grovehill, to the Whiting works off Queensgate on the west side of the town plus many others in between. Their warning sound was heard in every part of the town.

It was believed that the threat of incendiary bombs would be very real, with thousands of those bombs destined for homes and industry alike. To demonstrate the damage these bombs could cause and the effective measures that could be taken against extensive damage, three tables were erected each one with a top made of floorboards. The incendiary device on one was ignited which rapidly burned through the wood, falling to the ground and continuing to burn. At this point it was explained to the apprehensive audience that by spreading two inches of sand on the "upper floors" of their buildings, they could effectively prevent serious damage by fire; this was then demonstrated on the second table resulting in the wood under the sand only being singed.

The third demonstration showed how to smother an already burning device with sand and its subsequent removal.

In conclusion, the spectators were then shown the perils of throwing water over a burning incendiary bomb and the hazardous results caused by burning molten metal splattering and causing many smaller fires. The object of this exercise had been to bring to the public's attention the best way to deal with this type of fire without putting too much pressure on a Fire Brigade which would be stretched to the limit during an incendiary raid.

There followed a display by the auxilliary Fire Brigade who proudly showed under emergency conditions how they were able to lay a 100 feet of hosing and couplings in less than half a minute. They concluded by jetting water over the top of the Yorkshire Bank demonstrating that they could pump water up to the tallest building in the town. One wonders whether they were concerned at all about the town's much taller churches, including the Minster. Perhaps there would have been no chance of saving the Minster anyway, had it been bombed.

The final Fire Brigade demonstration of the evening probably presented the spectators with a scene reminiscent of Science Fiction comics or films, for looking as though they had just stepped from the pages or screen, came the gas decontamination squad. These "aliens" appeared as two wardens dressed in yellow oilskins comprising of trousers tucked in rubber boots, tightly fastened at the waist and wearing long sleeved coats of the same material tucked into gloves. Other equipment included service respirators and capes made from heavy oilskin. (What now follows may generate a chuckle, it did with me, for this I apologise).

The procedure was that in the event of a gas attack one warden was expected to phone for the decontamination squad, whilst his colleague went off to sound his "corn cake" (football rattle), to warn people of the presence of gas in the streets. It was envisaged that the decontamination squad would arrive on the scene "promptly" from their base behind the public baths, instructions dictating that their lorry complete with equipment should be parked safely upwind of the gas. The contaminated area would then be cordoned off, this being of paramount importance.

Bleaching powder (chloride of lime) was available to decontaminate, and the affected area would then be saturated with water, covered with a thick layer of bleach and the liquid flushed down the drains.

As will be appreciated the men in these airtight decontamination suits, became quite hot, "so the squad firemen rotated the men frequently to avoid fatigue and overheating"!

From the demonstrations and explanations the attendant public were now aware of these potential terrors, and were somewhat reassured in the knowledge that a team of trained personnel were on hand to assist whenever possible. However, the town was still in need of a 100 air raid wardens of whom it was expected 40 per cent would be women. It was hoped that from those who had turned out to the Market Place on that chilly night some would be tempted to become wardens and help to meet the required figures.

**"BE PREPARED"** was the scouts motto and to achieve this aim in the event of war, anti-gas training was offered to them. The younger boys were not left out; they could have an opportunity of being Scout Messengers. On Monday March 6th, the Rover Scouts had their first anti-gas training session.

On March 15th the Germans occupied Czechoslovakia; meanwhile a stranded whale occupied the beach at Flamborough. News of this was passed to the Bridlington Coastguards and upon their arrival they were surprised to see the whale about 100 yards off shore swimming about quite happily.

Unfortunately the poor creature grounded again and although still alive the coastguards claimed it for the "Crown". Apparently any whales that came ashore were classed officially as "shipwrecks" and as such had to be claimed.

Towards the end of May, in an experiment to test the effectiveness of a black-out in Beverley and District, everyone in the area was requested to ensure that their lights were either extinguished or effectively screened with blinds or dark curtains. The public were re-assured that electricity supplies would not be cut, but because of the restricted street lighting, vehicles were advised to keep off the roads if possible. But in the event of the "weather being unfavourable" the "Black-out" would be postponed!

From "Black out" doors to black indoors, and at the Beverley Regal their programme included a very thought provoking film entitled "Warning". This was a dramatic and informative production demonstrating what to do in the event of air raids should enemy aircraft drop incendiary bombs or gas.

However, the potential enemy were keen to "help" us in the event of a war, for a German manufacturer of Air Raid Shelters was advertising its products for sale to British people! I wonder did they come complete with guarantee and would it be possible to claim against the goods not standing up to "fair wear and tear"?

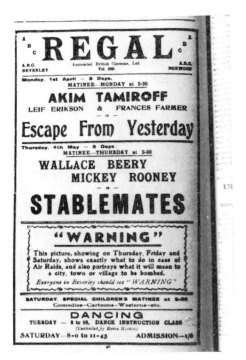

*Regal Cinema Programme,*
*April/May 1939.*

But what about all those German made hurricane lamps used in the black-out tests?!

A 61 year old Beverley man appeared at the Sessions House on a charge of being "drunk on a pedal cycle". He told the Magistrate he had learned his lesson and said "It's disgraceful for a man of my age. I have decided that I shall have to give up". The judge gave a smile of relief thinking the man meant drink, but then he added "cycling"!

It wasn't a drink problem for members of the Special Constabulary, but keeping their A.R.P. armbands up was. This became very apparent at the National Service Parade on the last Wednesday in June, for it was noticed that at least one man had marched part of the distance looking as though he had a stiff arm, his band gradually slipping over his wrist. In fact it was suggested that to alleviate this problem the A.R.P. should supply some "gold safety pins".

Within the first week of July, Beverley Borough Council had finalized their scheme for the reception and billeting of evacuees from Hull should war break out. The scheme included details of payment for billeting evacuees and what the payments would provide. School children were the first consideration. The expected number arriving in Beverley over the planned two days was to be 1,136 children and 114 teachers and helpers. A further 565 children along with 55 teachers and helpers would go to various parts of the Beverley Rural District.

The second day it was envisaged that 1,250 mothers and young children would arrive for Beverley, while the rural district would accommodate 620 mothers and children. This influx to the town and district would be on three trains from Hull on each of the two days and each child arriving was expected to bring a "bundle" holding a gas mask, change of clothes etc. The list reads as follows: "a change of underclothing, night clothes, house shoes, spare stockings or socks, a toothbrush, comb, towel and handkerchiefs and a warm coat or mackintosh, plus sufficient food for that day." (In cases where parents could not provide these items, reassurance was given to householders that they would not be expected to provide for them).

Mothers who would have similar burdens, and possibly young children, were instructed not to bring anything that couldn't be carried by hand.

Many householders had for some time wondered just what payments they could expect for taking in these unfortunates; after all additional mouths to feed and bodies to accommodate would cost money.

The Town Clerk provided a reasonable answer. For single unaccompanied children, the allowance would be 10/6 per week, where more than one child was taken, then it was 8/6 per child per week.

Children who were not old enough for school and would most likely be accompanied by their mothers or suitable guardian, would in this situation entitle the householder to receive 5/- a week for each adult, along with 3/- for the child.

Even though a state of readiness existed in the event of war, the vast majority of people never thought it would happen; but the time was drawing close.

Affording escapism from daily routine and a chance to "see the interesting sights of East Yorkshire", a Mystery Treasure Hunt was organized on July 25th in aid of the Cottage Hospital. All those participating (with the exception of

*Beverley Cottage Hospital "Treasure Hunt", July 1939.*

drivers) would donate 2/- in support of Hospital funds, but the event had to be postponed as it coincided with A.R.P exercises. However, this was only a temporary setback, for on the following Monday, July 31st, over 50 people took part in the treasure hunt and during $2\frac{1}{2}$ hours and over forty miles later most of the participants were reported to have had a " most enjoyable time". Little did they realize that in the not too distant future restrictions on petrol would outlaw this joyriding.

During late August some of the London museums and Art Galleries had closed to enable staff to pack national treasures in preparation for their removal and transportation to safety in different parts of the country.

For almost a year householders had been encouraged to build up food stocks, but as the prospect of war crept closer the demand on retail stocks had increased to a very noticeable level, bringing an appeal from the North Eastern Divisional Food Officer for people not to buy "beyond their usual needs".

The Post Office wasn't without problems, for their experts were desperately trying to trace a secret wireless station that was broadcasting "Don't fight" propaganda announcements.

The international situation was looking bleak and the belief that it would soon degenerate into something on the level of a disaster had prompted much activity in Beverley, and no doubt throughout the Country, as soldiers and airmen returned to their bases from broken leave.

A couple of interesting stories regarding the evacuees appeared in the Beverley Guardian's Beaver Column on September 9th and are worthy of inclusion.

The first tells of a well-known business man who had taken two young Hull boys into his house; he gave them threepence each and off they went to play on the Westood. One of the boys lost twopence and upon returning told of his loss to the business man's wife. Naturally she enquired who had given him the money, to which he replied "That there bloke that lives with you!"

The second relates how two young boys aged about seven or eight sat down to an attractive meal prepared with care by the lady who had taken them in, but to her distress they refused to eat it, and no matter how she tempted them, they preferred bread and butter. For tea they wanted bread and butter again and water instead of tea!

Throughout that last week of peace, each evening a team of volunteers had worked frantically filling sand bags to protect one of the most important buildings in the town, the Cottage Hospital.

The numerous windows had to be protected, a job which required 10,000 bags to be filled with sand and an appeal was made for more volunteers to work the weekend.

The town was saddened by news that a Territorial despatch rider had been killed at the North Bar when his motorcycle collided with a lorry. It was thought the accident may have been attributable to the masked traffic lights and that the unfortunate rider hadn't seen or misunderstood the light. The jury returned a verdict of misadventure adding that a sign placed on the road before the lights advising that "Dimmed traffic lights" were ahead would be an asset.

The Mayor, Councillor Arthur Watts, assured readers of the Beverley Guardian that Air Raid precautionary measures in the town were well in hand. Again a call for A.R.P. volunteers went out; 50 were still required to bring the Service up to its required strength.

The Borough Surveyor had deployed his staff in preparation for the black-outs. The department had acquired a new machine that enabled white lines to be marked on the roads, kerbstones had been painted white and the traffic lights at North Bar had been covered, with the exception of a small cross in the centre, thus allowing the colours to be seen safely without projecting a beam of light. Shopkeepers with illuminated display and neon signs had agreed not to use these during the hours of darkness.

September 1st, and Germany invaded Poland, bombs fell and Hitler's army moved in; our Government was obliged by a treaty to support Poland and in consequence issued an ultimatum demanding a German withdrawal. Its tolerance of Hitler's actions had come to an end.

The Beverley Guardian for Saturday September 2nd carried a report on the arrival of the "pathetic evacuees" that had arrived in Beverley the day previous. Many of these were children of five and six years old from the poorer areas of Hull, whom were felt could be vulnerable in the event of air attacks. The youngsters clutched tightly to their bags of food and clothing and at the same time gripped the person next to them as they marched from the Railway Station to the Square outside. It was noticed that they rarely smiled, but what was there to smile at. These little ones had been parted from there parents earlier that day and although within those young minds there may have been excitement and wonder, there was sadness in generous proportions. No doubt the accompanying teachers would face numerous problems in the weeks that followed. From the Station Square the evacuees were then taken to their respective schools, which were used as billeting centres for them, and given "mugs of steaming cocoa or tea".

It wasn't just art treasures that had to be preserved and protected from war, but history as well, so on Wednesday August 30th almost 2,000,000 feet of valuable historical film was transported to safety in Sussex from the National Film Library. Films included were the Funerals of Queen Victoria and King Edward VIII, the Coronation of King George VI and Queen Elizabeth, the Coronation procession of King George V, and troops going out to the Boer and Great Wars; the next historical event for the film cameramen would be without doubt the events over the next few years of this inevitable war.

Again from Joan Veitch are more memories, this time her last summer holiday told in her own words.

"The summer before war broke out, I had just had my thirteenth birthday. Suspecting that it might be the last real holiday for a long time, my parents rented a small house in Scarborough and a beach chalet for a whole month. Mother, myself and my two younger brothers were to stay the month (Adolf willing) and my father, who only got a fortnight's holiday from work, was to take us, stay the weekend and the last two weeks. We had a Scottish terrier, who of course was called Scottie, and he came with us too in our sturdy Morris Minor, bought second-hand and capable of reaching fifty miles an hour! It was black, with green leather seats.

We went long walks on the beach and the cliffs. Our amusements were simple and inexpensive. We had our wooden beach chalet with seats, a kettle and gas ring and, I think, a cold tap, or did we use a standpipe? Anyway, there was a block of toilets nearby. We were there for the whole day, every day. I made a collection of the wild flowers growing on the cliffs. I had a box of Reeves paints and tried to paint both Scalby Mills to the north and the old castle to the south. We paddled, collected sea shells and bathed when it was warm enough.

Each day the newspaper and radio gave graver and graver news, the German army was on manoeuvres and was massing near the Polish border. Mother, having experience of the last war, tried to calm my fears. "There won't be war till they've got the harvests in," she said, with the conviction of a countrywoman, "They need the harvest to feed the army, and the people at home".

I read my paperback Agatha Christies, priced 6d, old money, and old books I had bought for 2d at the second-hand stall. I took Scottie for long walks. But I knew, as everyone did, war was coming. I had grieved at Chamberlain and his "peace in our time". I felt we had betrayed Czechoslovakia. I could not know how unprepared the country was for war. But now German troops were invading Poland.

. Mother remembered the First World War, when two of her brothers had been in the trenches, and she had helped Belgian refugees who had settled in her quiet country village. She remembered the food shortages, and she had three young children to bring up. My father would not get his holiday in Scarboro' this year, or for many more years. Mother got out our trunks and started packing. I was given a task that was much to my sweet-toothed liking; the radio was giving government advice: each house should have a stock of food, not too much, for hoarding could be counted as a war crime. The bill boards at the time were full of the nutritional value of Cadbury's milk chocolate, each bar containing as much as two poached eggs and a pint and a half of milk. Scottie and I went into every sweet shop in Scarborough we could find to buy half-pound blocks of milk chocolate with all the money that should have been spent on our next fortnight's holiday. It seemed a lot of money and Scarboro' had a lot of sweet shops — but I persevered.

The lovely lights along the seafront that had danced and reflected themselves in the sea, went out. The whole town was in darkness. War had not yet been declared, but we knew Hitler could and would attack without warning or formal declaration of war.

The next day I tried to paint a picture of the castle; it had survived a lot of wars. Old and battered as it was, it would survive this one and I felt, after the war, I would come back and greet it as an old friend that had survived.

Saturday came and father would arrive. We went down to the beach for the last time. I noticed there was something different about the cars — the engines had a different note. Normally, in 1939 gears were changed quietly, slowly. Now the tension everyone felt meant that gears were changed rapidly, the accelerators were pressed down hard, and the engine revved up quickly. To me it was the most noticeable sign of the times. All the cars were heading inland and the beach was almost deserted. Some groups of evacuees wandered around sadly. Mother and other women discussed the stupidity of sending them to the coast for safety.

Father arrived at lunchtime. He was tired and unwilling to turn straight round and take us home, but mother insisted. After a quick sandwich lunch we were on our way. Father had been working very late every night at the office. All the important papers had had to be hand-copied, and the duplicates sent to a place of safety in case of the office being bombed. He had joined the A.R.P. and having been a soldier in the First World War realized how outnumbered our forces were, and how ill-equipped compared to the Germans. Hitler had chosen guns, not butter, for his country. Our politicians had allowed us to go on eating butter, rather than spend money on the forces. Now our young men were going to have to pay the price.

Already there was talk of petrol rationing and everyone was trying to keep their car tanks full. My father had cans of petrol in the boot in case we could not buy enough to get us home. He and mother discussed buying us all bikes whilst there were still some to be bought. If the Germans invaded, we would then be mobile. He would buy a cobbler's last too, and a stock of leather to keep our shoes in good repair.

When we got home, the house had a strange look. Father had nailed rugs and blankets across the windows as a makeshift black-out, though he then made a valuable discovery. The old Victorian villa we lived in had wood panels at the side of the glass windows. Father had cut through years of paint and discovered beautifully-fitting hinged wooden shutters which closed across inside the glass and were fastened with a strong iron bar. Not only were they light-proof, they were thick and strong enough to prevent splinters of broken glass flying in if we had a near miss. They gave me a great sense of security. All mother could think of was the mess of old paint on the carpet — father hadn't got round to sweeping it up!

The next morning, Sunday the 3rd of September, we gathered round the radio and heard Neville Chamberlain's speech declaring that this country was now at war with Germany. He sounded tired, almost listless, not an inspiring speaker, or leader, I felt. Nobody spoke for a moment, then normal life went on. Mother went into the kitchen to see to the Sunday lunch, father went into the yard to tinker with his car, and I went upstairs to finish my unpacking."

If you had kept up your payments to Briggs and Powell, you could hear on your own Murphy wireless the Prime Minister, Neville Chamberlain, speak to the nation. At 11.15 on the morning of Sunday September 3rd, he made the following historic announcement:

24

"I am speaking to you from the Cabinet Room at 10 Downing Street. This morning the British Ambassador in Berlin handed the German Government a final note, stating that unless we heard from them by 11 o'clock that they were prepared at once to withdraw their troops from Poland, a state of war would exist between us. I have to tell you that no such undertaking had been received and that consequently this country is at war with Germany."

The broadcast was heard by millions, and although expected over the previous few days, the declaration came as a strange sort of relief, breaking months of tension in anticipation of war. The announcement filled some people with pride, but at the same time a sadness with thoughts of the death and destruction that lay ahead. Others felt stunned in disbelief that the storm clouds of war had finally arrived to blot out the sun on that idyllic September Sunday.

Though the tranquillity of mind continued in many people, there was still a very real underlying threat of gas attacks and bombing raids. It was also feared that throughout the country half a million people would be killed in the first few weeks of the anticipated attacks and as well as the distribution of gas masks to everyone, preparations had been made by the government for *papier maché* coffins and mass burials.

Thankfully the gas attacks never came, but the bombs did, bringing with them their own horror.

The prospect of real war came within 12 hours of its declaration. The population were aroused from their slumbers by the wailing of the town's air raid sirens. Many awoke with sudden realization and fear that the dangers they had been taught to anticipate and prepare for could now be overhead and upon them within minutes. Grabbing gas masks some people foolishly rushed out into the streets, others sought safety under stairs, in cellars or wherever they felt safe.

As the drone of the bombers approached and receded, a sense of relief prevailed. This had been the first air raid and thankfully without incident. The bombers overhead had been our own returning from a propaganda leaflet dropping mission on Germany.

Hull's first Air Raid warning came at 3.20 a.m. on September 4th, with all operational staff taking their posts. This warning also passed without incident, though it was thought by some that the alarm was not necessary and someone may have nervously over-reacted.

The first weekend after the declaration of war, the Richardson family were to lose their lawn. It had been decided that it must go to make way for an air raid shelter. Mr Richardson, Beverley painter and decorator, lived with his family in a house at the Butcher Row end of Walkergate and the fact that they had a substantial lawn made this an ideal site for a shelter, and in that one weekend with help, the task was complete.

"The Richardson Shelter" had two entrances, was fully boarded out, had shelves, and afforded the 'luxury' of a primus stove.

It was decided that when the town's sirens were sounded, the factory hooters and buzzers should accompany them, practically guaranteeing that no-one in the town could fail to hear the warnings. As this was a sure way of getting people out of their beds, someone suggested (although I cannot think seriously) that when the war was over it might be worthwhile for the larger factories to sound their hooters and buzzers about threequarters of an hour before their workers were due to start, thus attempting to ensure better time keeping. But what about the disturbance to those who had no need to be awakened? Most people would have been unhappy at hearing that din in peacetime at 5.15 a.m. for the 6 a.m. starters!

Plans had already been prepared for petrol rationing. Until September 16th car owners were able to obtain petrol freely providing of course it went directly into the cars tank, with the recommendation that the car was used for essential purposes only.

Petrol rationing books were at the ready, with the first issue of coupons covering a period between September 16th and November 15th. Those days of carefree joyriding had at last come to an end.

With Art treasures and films hopefully protected from war damage or destruction, thoughts had turned to removing the valuable stained glass from the York Minster windows and by September 16th the 'Five Sisters' window had been removed and taken to safety. But with 113 windows containing stained glass, the task was enormous. Besides the glass, other treasures such as manuscripts normally kept in the library were removed and placed in fireproof safes which offered the added protection of being embedded in several feet of stone.

Those respected guardians of the black-out, the air raid wardens, who wasted no time in telling others that they had a light leak, were themselves victims of criticism for it had been noticed by many people in Grovehill Road that the wardens allowed light to shine through the bottom of the door of their post each night, and on one occasion when everyone should have been taking shelter, the door of the wardens post was wide open allowing a bright beam of light to shine across the road. I hope someone reminded them to practice what they preached!

While on the subject of black-outs, I feel it would be opportune to explain in more detail the difficulties this inconvenience caused, supported by two accounts from people who got lost in the black-out. Yet even with these personal insights, I find it hard to comprehend just how the population managed to exist without lights throughout the restrictive periods, but somehow they did!

I am amazed by the courage and confidence the public had in going out during the black-outs, especially women who repeatedly tell of the total lack of fear they had when walking the darkened streets. As a couple of them have remarked, how much safer they felt then, than they ever would now, even with the streets illuminated.

Many older readers will without doubt remember that, and even to permit the smallest chink of light to escape from your curtains or blinds would bring the wrath of the air raid warden to your door and a possible appearance in court if you failed to comply with regulations. Many, by virtue of their age, will find black-outs difficult to comprehend, as I did. The black-out started on September 1st 1939 a couple of days before the war was actually declared and continued, although with fewer restrictions, until May 1945.

It was a strange, but primitive belief, that if your enemy couldn't see you, he couldn't hurt you and so the black-out came into being. Laughable as it may sound, it was thought by some that even a lighted cigarette or upturned face could give sufficient guidance for enemy aircraft to attack!

But what an inconvenience the black-outs were, being immensely disliked by practically everyone. Just think of the problem of having to cover every window in the home with shutters, blinds or heavy curtains. Imagine the task in a building the size of the Beverley Arms Hotel (without extension) and that ritual had to be performed within half an hour of sunset every night! By the time restrictions eased, that tedious chore would have been carried out almost 2,000 times!

It was of course impossible to black-out buildings such as the Minster and St Mary's Church, so in the case of the latter they transferred evening service during the winter months, to the Playhouse Cinema. This venue proved very popular, possibly due to more comfort and warmth and being available to the congregation. At numerous services, even with extra chairs added, many people were turned away.

At this point I feel a need to satisfy the readers' curiosity by comparing the Cinema's role as a church with that of a "normal" church. While the congregation was arriving, sacred music was played over the Cinema's loudspeakers, the organist from St Mary's played the piano for hymns and psalms, and the choir sang from the front stalls. An additional benefit of these services was the hymn words projected onto the screen.

*Picture Playhouse  Advertisement  September 1939.*

'Black-out' literally meant 'black-out', so how did people move around? Well, with great difficulty, often resulting in people walking into each other, and of course every day street objects. These hazards were somewhat alleviated with the application of white paint round trees, lamp-posts, post boxes, kerb edges, street corners and vehicle mudguards.

Initially torches were banned, as were car headlights; this was the cause of numerous accidents (proved by Government Statistics) and during the first four months of the war, 1 in 5 people sustained an accident as a result of the black-out.

These restrictions were altered, allowing vehicles the use of headlights providing they were suitably masked and only a narrow beam of light illuminated the road ahead. At this time it became permissible to use a shrouded torch, that is of course if one could find the 'treasure' of a no.8 battery.

As you will have realized, the need for total darkness during the hours of darkness caused many problems especially to those people having to travel. It often proved to be a gamble, when it was only too easy to get on to the wrong train or bus. My mother and father travelling to York by train, suddenly realized a few miles from Beverley on the Scarborough line, that they were on the wrong track. Alighting at Arram station, they walked back to Beverley to start over again.

To be on the wrong bus or train was apparently quite commonplace, but just imagine being lost in your own town, a place you were familiar with well enough in daytime, but in a black-out..... This happened to Violet Moore. Upon leaving a friend's house, having talked and stayed too long, she walked a while in what she thought was the right direction, but soon realized she hadn't a clue where she was. Thankfully she noticed a man leaving a nearby house and approached him for help, admitting she was lost. Fortunately, he was heading towards Trinity Lane, and kindly offered to see her home to her house in nearby Eastgate.

Much concern had been expressed for old people living alone during air raids, many of whom were very frightened and upset when the warning sirens sounded, their loneliness adding greatly to their fear. One old lady awakened by the sirens sought shelter in the cupboard under the stairs, and there she stayed, crouched and shivering in the cold. Unfortunately, in her upset she had not heard the "all clear" sound and had remained under the stairs for many unnecessary hours until the milkman arrived and confirmed it was "all clear". Thankfully though the British Legion wardens and special constables were to work together in finding where old and lonely people lived, and after the "all clears" had sounded they would make visits to the elderly to check they were safe, hopefully avoiding a repeat of that poor lady's imprisonment.

The appeal earlier for help to fill the many sandbags for the protection of the Cottage Hospital had met with a good response. However the task was not complete and by mid September there were 2,000 bags still to fill; the appeal for volunteers went out again.

By the end of September there had been no air-raids, but the public were constantly reminded of the need to remain alert. At night they had to know where their shoes, clothes and gas masks were so that they could dress and equip in the dark as quickly as possible and to familiarize themselves with shortest and quickest routes to the nearest shelter.

Even without raids, the war brought distress to many who were unable to make ends meet as a result of the war taking away their livelihood. Thankfully the Ministry of Labour had provided for these people, but they had to prove they and any dependants were in need.

Britain as an island nation had to rely on large quantities of imported food. The war had brought about dramatic changes in its supply as ships ran the constant gauntlet of attack from German U-boats and what food was carried had to compete for hold space with the vital raw materials needed to fight the war. This resulted in the space for food diminishing while space for war materials expanded.

With this dramatic cut in imports, it became necessary for this Island race to become self-sufficient in food production.

Before the war, acres of the countryside had become neglected partly due to the growers' inability to compete with the vast quantities of cheap American grain which had forced the price of corn down to its lowest level in 300 years. This had caused many farmers to neglect their land and machinery. Many areas had become overgrown wildernesses. This was soon to change; every available acre of land had to be cultivated. To ensure that this was efficiently done, the Government established war agricultural committees to organize the farmers' productivity in each district with the support of government grants.

Horticulture came under critical review as it was deemed necessary to convert flower beds, lawns, grass verges and even window boxes for vegetable production. It was now a "dig for victory".

Flowers were to suffer most, perennials to be reduced by 30%, chrysanthemums were expected to be reduced by 50% in 1940, and so the list continued, including those under glass. Everyone was encouraged to utilize all land wisely for the propagation of essential food.

Local Authorities had been granted powers of access to land for growing food and their aim was to target 500,000 allotments. It was no good kicking up a fuss if you enjoyed that bit of grass across the road, because if the authorities wanted it and 'it' was unoccupied, then they could have it cultivated without consent. (Occupied land had to have permission from the owner first, and common land had to have the Minister's seal of approval).

Here in Beverley, parts of our beautiful Westwood were sacrificed for the growing of necessary crops and everyone was encouraged to prepare their own kitchen garden. Almost overnight Britain became a nation of gardeners.

The petrol restrictions were the reason for many people having to "lay up" their cars, but strange as it may seem, there was still a demand for cars. In fact one factory's production of 200 cars in the week had been taken by dealers who had customers waiting. Probably many of the higher-powered cars were being requisitioned by the authorities and their owners were replacing them with smaller and more economical models.

I wonder how the organisers of the Cottage Hospital "win a car" competition felt about the petrol situation. Mr Gordon Armstrong had kindly donated a Morris Eight Saloon valued at £128 as first prize. However, prospective entrants need not have been deterred, for the small print in the advert offered a cash alternative to the car's value.

Those who sold food required a licence, regardless of where it was sold from. Shops, hand carts, market stalls, all had to register with the Food Control Committee and they had forms for practically everything that passed the lips; for example for butter, margarine and other fats no less than six forms were involved.

However, there was no form-filling at the Salvation Army Harvest Festival. The children were again encouraged to bring along their decorated baskets of fruit and vegetables, which were then disposed of by sale, the proceeds benefitting the Army funds. This year one young girl not wanting to be left out, had taken along one small apple as her harvest gift; small as the apple was, its value was big — the apple was auctioned and raised 2/5.

"Someone has gone too far", that was the cry from the residents of Weel and rightly so, for someone decided that the Grovehill Ferry bridge over the River Hull must close each night at 7.00 p.m. "by order", instead of the usual 9.00 p.m. This caused immense inconvenience especially for those working in Beverley, for if they were a few minutes late the only alternative was a cycle ride or walk of a distance of five miles round by Hull Bridge. Even for motorists, that extra distance was a burden on the rationed petrol.

The decision to close the bridge had been made by one man, but the Town Council endorsed the decision.

However, it was eventually agreed that throughout the winter months, the bridge would still continue to close at 7.00 p.m. with the exception of Saturday nights when the opening would be extended until 9.00 p.m. And the reason behind this state of affairs? Well, it's those blackout restrictions again. You see, they didn't just apply to roads, but to rivers also. Therefore the river traffic was unable to display lights and of course neither was the Ferry Bridge. This in turn led to the bridge keeper being unable to tell when vessels were approaching. These restrictions outlawed the use of hooters and horns, so the poor chap would in darkness have no chance of removing the 'bridge' from the path of an oncoming vessel, which if hit would have effectively severed that link with Weel, making its residents even worse off than previously. And so it was that residents of Weel had no choice but to be home by 7.00 p.m. or 9.00 p.m. on Saturdays or face that long trek round by Hull Bridge to get home.

On the night of Sunday October 1st, the King signed a proclamation "calling-up" for National Service all men of 20 and 21 years of age. The proclamation indicated that with certain exceptions, all British males who were in the country on that date would be eligible for Military Service. This first call-up was to affect around 250,000 men in this age group. However it was felt that the next "call-up" affecting the following age group would not be required before the new year.

Every British citizen had to hold an Identity card, issued under the National Registration scheme. By the beginning of October a high percentage of the population had their cards, but the question was often asked "what is their purpose, what do we do with them?" The original plan had been that the cards could be used to help compile a complete record of the population for National Service purposes. However, at this time their main use was for support in the issue of ration books, although it was made quite clear on the cards that they could be required "under conditions of National emergency for important purposes". Whatever the reason, everyone had to have one.

On Monday October 2nd, the town magistrates dealt with their first cases under the black-out regulations. A Hull man was fined 10/- for not suitably obscuring the sidelights of his car, and a Beverley shop assistant received a 5/-fine through not having a rear red light on his cycle. No doubt there would be many more to follow.

On the Railways there were signs that slight improvements could be on the way to ease railway travel during the hours of darkness. It was hoped that the introduction of blue lights to passenger carriages would make travelling in total darkness a thing of the past.

By mid October it was reported that the town had been divided into 40 sections each containing about 100 houses. For each sector one Senior Warden had been appointed with four deputies under him. 14 warden posts had been established in positions affording the best areas of cover and although not fully equipped yet, it wouldn't be long before they contained everything from whistles to gum boots, anti-gas curtains to handbells, in fact all a warden would be likely to want.

15,000 gas masks had been assembled, and their distribution and demonstrations of fitting had been efficiently carried out by the wardens. School children were being taken to the gas chambers (don't be alarmed) for mask testing, for out of 1,300 tested, ten had been found faulty (although nine had not fitted properly).

The St Mary's Church services held in the Playhouse continued to be popular; in fact it was reported that the hall was usually filled by the time the services started.

Did you know it was forbidden to take a dog into a public air-raid shelter? Yes it was, and the Secretary of the National Canine Defence League appealed to dog lovers to offer refuge in their own shelters to those unfortunate enough to be out when the sirens sounded. To help, the League had prepared small signs for display indicating where dogs and their owners would be welcome to take shelter.

The argument over the early closing of the Weel/Grovehill Ferry Bridge continued into October. Mr Frank Ringrose, one resident of Weel who ran the town's Army and Navy store, expressed his annoyance at the Council's decision on the early closing of the Ferry Bridge. This had forced him to close his business at 6.45 p.m. each evening except Saturdays. His failure to reach the bridge in time would force him into making too long a journey home by Hull Bridge.

However, someone had pointed out that the closure of the Ferry Bridge and the fear of it being struck by river craft in darkness was quite unfounded, for since the outbreak of war no vessels were using the river, mainly because both the Sutton Road bridge in Hull and the Hull Bridge closed each evening at dusk!

Tuesday morning October 17th, brought Beverley's first daylight air raid warning. As the sirens relayed their cries, the streets began to clear, with people seeking safety, running to their homes or the nearest places of shelter. Children attending schools were sent home, but as some crossed the Market, it was noticed that there was no-one to guide them across this busy area. About the same time a more serious incident was taking place at the Cherry Tree railway crossing; on the town side of the crossing numerous school children cried, whilst on the other side mothers screamed in fear and panic, unable to reach their children. This continued for about 10 minutes as trains shunted backwards and forwards; eventually the signal man was told that an air raid was in operation and responded by holding up shunting operations thus allowing the frightened children to cross the lines to their distraught mothers.

Meanwhile back in the town centre, the initial reaction to the sirens had settled, and people curious to see what was going on started to venture outside again. The first noticed around the Market Place were the many butchers, probably more apparent by their "whites", but it wasn't long before other traders and their assistants appeared in small groups standing in their shop doorways and on the pavements. Wives of Market Place residents also came out, people were seen to point and look at the barrage ballons as they gently rose over Hull high into that October sky. Occasional vehicles still unaware of the raid passed through the town.

Then the sound of aircraft was heard, and probably with a mixture of fear and excitement, the many townspeople watched as three Spitfires passed over heading in a north-easterly direction. Everyone waited in anticipation of aerial action, while members of the Special Constabulary walked the streets warning and begging the people outside to take cover indoors, although few took any notice.

Soon after the Spitfires had passed, the sky was filled with many wings, but thankfully those of wild geese, as a large flock in excellent formation passed overhead. Suspicions that this had been a false alarm were soon confirmed and although causing a great deal of inconvenience, it had proved that the services were prepared even if the public didn't co-operate to the full. However, such problems as the school children crossing the town's Market and the Cherry Tree crossing incident along with the curiosity of the people to see what was going on outside did give cause for concern, the latter even to the point whereby the Chairman of the town's A.R.P. committee, Councillor C.H. Burden, broadcast an appeal over the Radio-by-wire the following evening, to the townspeople, urging them to take every precaution to protect themselves during air raids and not to remain on the streets at such times.

As if there were not enough existing problems in those troubled times, there was still time and energy for criticism of colleagues and in particular of the Head Air Raid Wardens. Sadly some people had "hinted and even asserted" that they had received "large payments" for their services. The Chairman of the A.R.P. Committee sprang to their defence through a letter to the Beverley Guardian, whereby he re-assured readers that the wardens had not, and did not, receive any payment whatsoever, and warned that such rumours, whether malicious or through ignorance, would unless suppressed result in the prosecutiuon of those guilty of spreading such stories.

Within the same column, two letters were printed both expressing concern over children being turned out of school when an Air Raid warning was sounded, with instructions for them to get home as fast as possible; not only were the children exposed to danger, but also those parents who went out to look for and meet them. These concerns were of particular relevance especially since only days before the A.R.P. Chairman had broadcast over the Radio his appeal for people to remain indoors during Air Raid warnings. One correspondent, a father himself, felt it would be better for the children to be kept in school until the danger passed and even though the parents would still be worried, at least they would have the satisfaction of knowing where their children were.

It was a great pity that all pet owners didn't always know or care where their pets were, especially at night during the black-out, many having become a nuisance to road users and pedestrians alike. It was incredible to think just how irresponsible some people could be, allowing their cats and dogs to roam the streets at night. They were easy prey for motorists, but even worse were the number of cyclists and pedestrians riding and walking into them, and adding to the problems, there was the additional hazard of dogs fouling the footpaths. Without doubt wartime streets at night did have their difficulties.

November 6th saw the commencement of "National Rat Week" when everyone was urged to destroy as many rats as possible. This move had been deemed necessary by the Ministry of Agriculture as a direct result of "serious depredations on food stocks by rats". Thankfully for anyone not quite sure how to "do it", a solution was at hand, as for 6d. it was possible to obtain the Ministry's Bulletin issue no.30 entitled "Rats and How to Exterminate them".

Returning to the Grovehill Ferry Bridge, the Town Council had thought the matter over, probably as a result of a deputation from concerned residents of Weel, and the outcome was that the bridge could remain open until 7.15 p.m. instead of 7.00 p.m. when light permitted. Then the original hours of closing would be resumed. The Borough Surveyor was authorised to provide improved facilities for the bridgeman so that he might safely pass from bridge to river bank. (Somehow this whole business appeared odd to say the least especially when River traffic posed no problem to the Ferry as none used this stretch of river at night anyway!)

With winter very much in mind, and the prospect ahead of fuel restrictions this was the time to prepare for colder weather, and so Messrs Reynolds on the Railway Street corner were in November 1939 offering slipovers, pullovers, jerseys and roll collar pullovers at attractive prices ranging from 1/11 to 12/11. Thoughts of Christmas came from Green's in the Market Place, offering a "splendid selection" of private Christmas cards with prices and designs to suit all tastes.

The blackouts continued to be a nuisance to everybody, pipe smokers having suffered more than cigarette smokers! as a direct result of walking into people. The main area of sufferance appeared to be the roof of their mouths, although one unfortunate chap had the stem of his pipe pushed down his throat, whilst the lady he collided with sustained a painful bruise on her nose, it being on the receiving end of his pipe bowl. The message to smokers was simple: if you must smoke stay indoors, or stick to cigarettes.

On December 1st, the proprietor of the Playhouse Cinema, Ernest Symmons, speaking at the Rotary Club meeting once again expressed concern over the necessity for air raid shelters in the town. He explained with diagrams how vulnerable Beverley was to air raid attack and how in 1938, when the war was not a reality, trenches had been dug in certain parts of the town; yet in 1939 when the war was actual, little was being done to provide any protection. He felt that shelters should be erected in the busiest areas of the town, so as to provide refuge for people well away from their homes. Mr. Symmons had acquired 400 signatures from people who also thought that public shelters were a necessity for the town.

It was a sad state of affairs to say the least. Some factories had at great expense provided shelters for their employees. Both the Girls High and Boys Grammar Schools were provided for, but for anyone out in the streets of Beverley, nothing! nor was there adequate shelter or protection for younger children attending the junior schools.

Do you recall that Cottage Hospital fund raising car competition held some time ago? Well petrol rationing or not, the car was won by Mr Shillito of Wombwell near Barnsley, and after expenses had been deducted, the Cottage Hospital benefitted by £128.

On Saturday December 23rd, the Beverley Guardian proudly displayed the headline "Air Raid Shelters for Beverley". At last Beverley would have shelters for the public. This was mainly due to Ernest Symmons who along with the Beverley Guardian and a few others, had gallantly and relentlessly campaigned for public shelters. It was hoped that by early 1940, few people using the town streets would be far from a shelter in the event of a raid.

Christmas entertainment at the Cinema brought Deanna Durbin to the Playhouse screen in "Three Smart Girls Grow Up", also a novelty film entitled "Audioscopics", which when viewed through the "Special Spectacles" allowed the viewer to see "figures on the screen become solid". And as there was a matinee at 2.30 on Christmas day, the Playhouse afforded that welcome post Christmas lunch sit down; and so the first Christmas of the war passed quietly, that is except for the traditional festive revellers some of whom of course supped too freely from the "cup that cheers".

# 1940 and Rationing

So the war wasn't over by Christmas as many had predicted and hoped it would be, and the question in the minds of many was just what would 1940 hold? One thing was certain: food rationing.

Christmas 1939 would probably have lingered in people's minds for many months, as they remembered the festive fare of that last Christmas before food rationing came into operation — on Monday January 8th 1940, introducing what soon became a priceless possession to all classes, 'The Ration Book'.

From this date the first items to be rationed were ham, bacon, sugar and butter. In March, meat became rationed by price, not weight, and July brought the traditional British brew, tea, into restriction, followed shortly by cheese, cooking fat, sweets and conserves. By 1944 11/- of every £1 spent on food was on rationed items.

By 1941 each adult was allowed the following quantities of rationed food per week:

Fat 8oz (226g) including 2oz Butter, Tea 2oz (57g), cooked meat a mere 2 slices, Ham 4oz (114g), Cheese 1oz (28g), Sugar 8oz (226g), Jam 2oz (57g), meat as much as one shilling would buy and one egg.

But whatever criticisms were raised about rationing, it was proved that with less fats, sugar and meat being consumed, the population of the country was healthier, especially with the increased intake of fruit and vegetables.

Evacuees hadn't been forgotten. One report told of Girl Guides who had sung Christmas carols over the festive period and raised £2-0s-0d. With the money a party was given and on Tuesday January 2nd, 24 children from the Wold Road area of Hull were entertained at the Tiger Lane rooms.

In the second week of the New Year, the call-up of the next age group of men was announced. This time it was for men in the 22-23 age group, and although they should have been called earlier, a promise had been given when they registered that Christmas and the New Year would be spent at home. No doubt thoughts of the next Christmas, and if they would be home to share it, must have crossed their minds.

Relief was felt by many parents of babies on hearing that the babies' Anti-gas helmets had at last arrived and were to be distributed, with demonstrations at the School Clinic.

Another problem of the black-out, and one not given much thought to other than by bus drivers, was that of negotiating the Beverley Bar after dark (many readers may not know, but the old East Yorkshire buses were built specially domed to fit neatly into and through the Bar's arch). Any driver who didn't get his aim right first time would invariably hit the arch brickwork and dint his bus roof, so imagine having to negotiate this obstacle at dark and in a black-out! Some bus conductors actually left the buses and "walked" them through, guiding the driver from the road in front. Then someone had a 'bright' idea, a small light was fitted into the top of the arch thus illuminating the inner sides of the bar, but not the roadway, and bringing great relief to the many drivers using the bar.

On January 20th, a public meeting was held in the Playhouse Cinema, when once again the question of Air Raid shelters was under review. Even with abysmal weather conditions, around a hundred people attended to hear points for and against Air Raid shelters being built for the public's safety. It would be expensive, but then what price a human life? In due course, shelters were built, but the subject lingered a long time under discussion, probably due in part to a belief that Beverley was not considered to be a danger zone.

On January 29th, snow fell causing severe drifting on the roads across the Westwood. Unfortunately the manpower required to deal with the blockage was deployed on the town's snowclearing. However, a call from the Borough Surveyor to the C.O. at the Barracks brought forth 60 soldiers to assist with the road clearance.

A bright spot in the winter gloom came in late February with the establishment in the Market Place of "The Pale Moon" canteen. This facility was provided by Mr Gordon Armstrong of Longcroft Hall, who generously offered free tea and coffee to everyone in uniform. It was welcomed by all who used it.

Did you know that if you defaced, destroyed or lost your ration book, the only way a replacement could be obtained was by payment of 1/- to the food control committee, and if your hobby was photography or even just a casual snapshooter, then care had to be exercised over what you photographed? However for a penny you could buy a copy of the "control of photographs" order which listed photographic forbidden objects.

The Rambla bakery declared that their bread was best: it "cuts well, keeps well" and "eats well", but for the home cook there was a recipe in the Beverley Guardian for a "War cake", still worthy of reproducing many years on:- "Two large cups of flour (plain), 1 cup sugar, 2oz shelled walnuts, 1 teaspoonful carbonate of soda, ½lb chopped dates, ½ pint milk, 1 teaspoonful baking powder, ¼lb margarine".
"Rub shortening into flour; add rest of ingredients, mixing in milk gradually. Bake in moderate oven for about an hour. Don't open the oven door until the cake has been in 40 minutes — this is important!"

How many readers remember that Beverley character George (Nixy) Oliver, who worked many years as a "news-vendor" for Atkinsons newsagents?

I have only a very vague recollection of George, but have heard it said that when selling certain women's magazines, he was often heard to ask if anyone wanted a woman! (and I believe George's sales of the sporting pink caused him a problem or two in a certain circle!) My memory of him is that of a short, stocky, baldish man with thick spectacles and ruddy complexion, but I'm sure there are readers of more mature years who will have better memories.

However, the reason for mentioning George is as a result of an appeal through the press by his employers for customers to call at their shop at 51 Toll Gavel to pay their papers, thus helping George by reducing the amount of walking he did in an attempt to help his recurring foot problems.

I was very pleased to have my memories of Nixy Oliver re-kindled and I hope by mentioning him in this book, many readers will share a thought for a once well-known and respected Beverley character.

"Waste material is War material" — this was the slogan people were asked to remember when discarding rubbish. The shortages brought about by war and very restricted imports made it essential to save waste and use everything to its fullest potential. Iron railings surrounding properties were seen as raw materials for the war effort and were requisitioned. Household waste was separated to provide swill for the pigs, paper to recycle, bones for glue making and cordite; in fact it was said that one chop was sufficient to make cordite for two gun cartridges; but amidst this utilization of waste, a shortage of kitchen utensils was created as millions of aluminium pans etc. were donated towards the building of aircraft. However, this aluminium salvage proved to be unnecessary as later it was revealed that sufficient aluminium scrap was already available.

Even though the black-out regulations had been in operation for some time, it appears that not everyone was fully conversant with them, as people were fined weekly for breaking the black-out, either with lights from homes, or vehicles, or as one man did, by lighting a bonfire. One chap was taken to task for not having his car bumpers and running board painted white!

On April 9th, Germany invaded Denmark and Norway. A patriotic note was sounded by the Spencer School Orange Day celebrations, when "little" Hilda Gillett sang a solo from the song "Keep right on to the end of the road". That particular Orange Day celebrated the anniversary of the birth of the school's founder. (Being an ex-pupil of that grand institution, I was interested to learn during researches that the first distribution of oranges had taken place on April 14th 1911. For those readers not familiar with the Spencer School's traditional Orange Day, the giving of an orange to each pupil was established as a result of a headmaster, a certain Mr Spencer, who had left £100 invested, the interest of which provided the money to purchase oranges each year).

Three cheers for the Beverley Dairymen, as they announced a reduction in the price of milk from Sunday May 5th until further notice. The price dropped to 3d per pint.

May 10th brought a change of Prime Minister and a coalition Government as Winston Churchill replaced Neville Chamberlain. On the same day Germany invaded Holland, Luxemburg and Belgium.

The long feared invasion of Holland, Belgium and Luxemburg brought an immediate wave of concern to the British public. The Whitsuntide Bank Holiday was cancelled along with the Beverley Races. The public were urged to carry their gas masks with them on all occasions. Almost daily the war was getting nearer to our shores, provoking the need to remind people during a raid to avoid sight-seeing, to keep clear of windows, and to leave doors unlocked, so that those unfortunates caught out in a raid might seek refuge indoors.

On May 13th the Germans attacked France at Sedan. The following day May 14th brought the first call for Local Defence Volunteers. This was to be a volunteer group functional throughout the county to effectively handle possible parachute attacks.

In Beverley six weddings had been cancelled as the worsening international situation put a stop to the bridegrooms' leave. Unaffected, the Minster Garden Party went ahead on the vicarage lawn. A patriotic touch came with the Union Jack proudly displayed in the centre of the lawn. The event was opened by Lady MacDonald of the Isles.

By late May, it looked as though those public Air Raid shelters were at last becoming a reality as the Council approved the provision of shelters which could accommodate 1,500 people, and the cost? Around £6,000! Forget the cost, and have a laugh at the Pictures, for on the bill was 'A Real Cure For The Black-Out Blues' in "Old Mother Riley Joins Up".

By May 26th, British troops were trapped at Dunkirk and the evacuation of them began.

Car owners had something to moan about, as the much valued petrol increased in price again, the fourth time in nine months! This time it was by $1\frac{1}{2}$d bringing the cost of a gallon up to 1s.$11\frac{1}{2}$!

Although neutral at the outbreak of war, on June 19th Italy declared war on France and Britain. The same day the RAF station at Leconfield was the target for some of Hitler's high explosive bombs. Fortunately four landed in a nearby field and only one on the aerodrome. There were no casualities, athough some buildings were slightly damaged.

Work, although slow, had at last started on building the public shelters. July brought the introduction of Domestic Shelters. These would be Do-It-Yourself jobs with the Government funding them through local Councils by providing the necessary materials for the householder to construct his own shelter. However if his income was in excess of £250 per annum, then a contribution of £7 was expected towards the cost.

*George (Nixy) Oliver.*

*The Beverley War-time Day Nursery in 1940. The three adults (left to right) are Kathleen Bell, Lorna Allison and Miss Clarkson. The children include the following: Michael Partridge, Colin and Thelma Johnson, Brian Gillet, Adrian Middleton and Louis John.*

# Someone here is going to need your help

Johnny lives in the city. His home may seem safe enough now. But if raids come it will be another matter. Johnny must be moved. It is unthinkable that he should be left to take his chance among the horrors of modern bombing warfare.

The Government is going to send Johnny to your district if raids come. This is where your help is needed. To promise now to give Johnny a home, so that the authorities may know he will be cared for. Do not think that because we have not been raided yet, we are not likely to be.

As the year grows older the danger does not grow less. These children in the city may be needing a safe home next month, next week, perhaps tomorrow. When they do, they will need it suddenly, urgently, desperately.

All you need do is enrol your name with your local Authority. You may be asked to take a child now, or your name may be kept against the time when raids make a second evacuation necessary. When you enrol, you will be doing a splendid service for the nation.

**The Minister of Health, who has been entrusted by the Government with the conduct of evacuation, asks you urgently to join the Roll of those who are willing to receive children. Please apply to your Local Council.**

*Evacuee Advertisement "Someone here is going to need your help", from the Beverley Guardian, 6th April 1940.*

*Bomb damage in Summergangs Road, Hull, 26th June 1940. Photo by courtesy of City of Hull Record Office.*

*Hull's Wilfreds Terrace air raid shelter, situated between two rows of terraced houses, 7th July 1940. Photo by courtesy of City of Hull Record Office.*

*Bomb damage to shops in Great Passage Street, Hull, 30th July 1940. Photo by courtesy of City of Hull Record Office.*

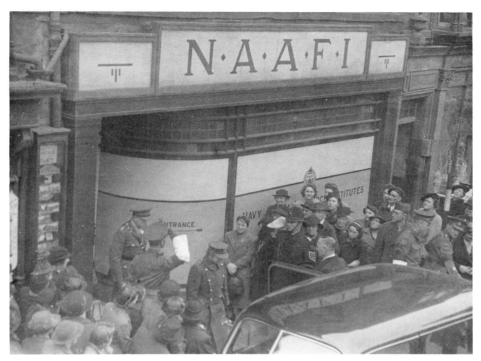

*H.R.H. the Princess Royal visits the NAAFI in Beverley on 9th August 1940.*

*Bomb damage to a house and shops in Holderness Road, Hull, on 25th August 1940. Photo by courtesy of City of Hull Record Office.*

*Two men look on at the rubble of what was a house in Hull, Autumn 1940.
Photo by courtesy of City of Hull Record Office.*

On July 4th, British Somaliland was invaded by Italy.

The weather wasn't all it could be for a so-called summer (some things never change), as heavy rain caused serious flooding in Beverley. The complaints weren't about the quantity of water, but more the inadequacy of the town's ancient drains to cope with the volume. Back to those public shelters, and at last many were ready for use, but children were being a bit of a nuisance (as I've said some things never change); the little rascals had evolved a new pastime and were beating Hitler to it by partially demolishing the escape walls.

The possibility of an invasion by the enemy of our Yorkshire Coast could not be ignored; the official advice to the public was to "stay put", but should the roads become clogged with refugees fleeing inland, then civil and military authorities would take any action necessary to prevent not just the refugees, but vehicles, from blocking the roads. However, in issuing these statements, it was emphasized that there was no need to panic or assume that an invasion was imminent even though the enemy was getting nearer.

At 11.13 p.m. on June 19th, the first "incident" within Hull's City boundary was reported when as a result of incendiary bombs being dropped, a fire was started in Marfleet. Just over an hour later, parts of East Hull were showered with incendiary bombs, thankfully resulting in little damage.

Hull can also claim another first, the City being the victim of the country's first daylight raid. This took place on July 1st when an enemy aircraft crossed Hull, apparently unnoticed, that is until it was too late for a warning to be sounded and by that time it had struck the Saltend Oil Refinery resulting in five fires being started.

In late July a warning was made to sightseers of bomb damage. This was directed at those wishing to inspect bomb craters in fields of crops (other than grass) due to the excessive damage sightseers could do. In one case 25 acres of wheat had been damaged, not by enemy action but by people tramping on it to look at a crater. So, any person found guilty of this sort of destruction could be fined up to £50.

Concern for the removal and storage of Beverley Minster's priceless East window continued to bring in donations, the estimated cost of the work being £550. Towards the end of July £56-3-0 had been raised; still with windows, but on the domestic front, it was possible to buy "Anti-Splinter" nets for sticking on windows. They were cheap and simple to fix; all that was required was cutting to size (allowing for slight shrinkage) moistening and then just putting in place. Repeated tests had proved their effectiveness in reducing the danger of flying glass splinters, and into the bargain they looked quite attractive.

More generosity came from Mr Gordon Armstrong, this time in the way of a donation of £8,500 to the Nation for the purchase of a Spitfire or Hurricane and the use of his residence, Longcroft Hall, as a Hospital for the duration of the War.

August 9th brought a visit from HRH the Princess Royal to Beverley. The occasion of this Royal visit to the WVS premises was recorded on film by Proprietor of the Playhouse cinema, Ernest Symmons, and was shown at his cinema in the popular Playhouse news, to appreciative audiences.

Grace Martin lives in Rudston, a few miles north east of Driffield, and she recalls her wartime memories. Her father was a coal merchant, but due to shortages of manpower Grace was obliged to help with the family business, the duties of which included 'leading' coal from Burton Agnes station, filling the sacks and then delivering them. I was quite surprised to learn from Grace that the then small village of Rudston hosted a German Prisoner of War Camp and hospital!

Grace was married on February 17th 1940, her husband being a rear-gunner flying in Whitley bombers stationed at Driffield. Their wedding was the first military wedding ever held in the Rudston church.

However, Rudston didn't escape the war completely unscathed by enemy action, for the village was the recipient of "gifts" from Hitler in the shape of "heavy bombs" that fell in and around it. Luckily no-one was killed or injured, but the bombs caused substantial damage and started a few fires.

Whilst in the area I feel this would be a suitable place to mention the Driffield airfield, which originally dated back to 1918. The new airfield was opened as a bomber station on July 30th 1936 with the aircraft arriving in September. Driffield is noted for being the first operational station against the enemy, their first mission taking place on the nights of September 4th and 5th 1939.

On August 15th 1940 Driffield became victim of a severe attack by the enemy. They made their approach near Flamborough Head in the late morning. Radar picked up the aircraft but they separated into 8 groups, adding to the confusion. The main party targetted Driffield. A hundred and sixty nine bombs were dropped and the resulting damage was extensive. The airfield was a mass of bomb craters which alone made the station unoperational up to the year end. Twelve Whitley bombers were totally destroyed and four hangars suffered cannon and bomb damage. Obviously the decoy airfield at nearby Skerne had had no effect on this occasion, but in an attempt to fool enemy reconnaissance dummy aircraft were placed on the airfield once the damaged real ones had been removed. Their position was changed each night so that the airfield looked operational.

Still with East Yorkshire airfields, but a few miles south west and over the Wolds to Pocklington. This was one of the airfields destined by the RAF for upgrading as a bomber base. Although this decision was made around 1935, work didn't commence until very late in 1939. Completed, Pocklington opened in the June of 1941 as a bomber station along with a decoy field at nearby Burnby. Doreen Clark lived on a farm five miles away from Pocklington, her bedroom facing in that direction. She recalls one night just as it was getting dusk seeing a plane on fire coming in to land. The next thing Doreen saw was a bright flash followed a few seconds later by a loud explosion that rattled her bedroom window.

A great many of Doreen's schooldays were spent living at her Grandparents, then home for weekends — this was due to school being nearer and more convenient. In her Grandparents' village an air raid siren was mounted on the public house chimney stack and when it sounded Doreen sought refuge under the table while her Grandparents remained seated quite unperturbed in their respective seats on either side of the fireplace. You see Grandad would never take shelter, so Grandma always sat with him to keep him company!

With the war now a year old and winter ahead bringing long nights of black-out, the Playhouse Cinema at the end of September again took on the role of church, hosting the congregation of St. Mary's Church.

From 'down under' comes Ron Thompson's wartime memory. Ron, now living in Queensland, Australia, told of the night he was at the Playhouse when suddenly the main film stopped and the cinema proprietor, Mr Symmons, announced "... that he had just heard on the radio that our airforce had that day shot down a huge number of enemy aircraft over Southern England. The audience all cheered, a few people left, but most of us remained to see the rest of the film." Apparently the Battle of Britain was at its height.

In the meantime the Mayoress, Mrs Arthur Watts, was appealing for help to unaugurate a fund eventually to buy a spitfire aeroplane in token of the town's support towards the war effort.

Saturday September 7th saw the start of the "Blitz" on London, the first daylight raid being responsible for the deaths of 400 people.

By mid September, the funds for the removal and safe storage of the Minster's East window stood at £227-12-9, almost half the original target and the Mayoress's Fighter Fund, growing daily, had reached £336-0-8. The public

46

were encouraged to think "A Spitfire a day keeps 'Jerry' away"!

In an attempt to hide from the enemy, many factories were being camouflaged and so thoughts turned to hiding the town's two large churches, the Minster and St. Mary's. But just how would you begin to camouflage those enormous towers? Needless to say they never were.

September 15th brought bombing attacks on London of an unprecedented severity. A day later on the 16th, conscription came into operation in the United States.

Violet Moore, like so many wives and mothers throughout the country, had to spend most of the war without her man around the home. Ted Moore, already an AA Patrolman, was given the option of being a despatch rider or Special Constable. Ted chose to be a despatch rider and as such, with the exception of leave, he spent most of six years away from his wife and children.

In this real war situation, over and above the natural panic associated with the wailing sirens and their warnings, chaos ensued as people rushed to the relative safety of the shelters. Violet remembers well the night she hadn't heard the sirens and was awakened by her neighbours knocking at her door and saying "this was going to be a bad one", judging by the sound of the bombers coming. Hastily grabbing her three children, she made off through an orchard in the darkness to the sanctuary of the Eastgate shelter. On arrival she discovered that she had run the distance barefoot, but in the panic hadn't noticed. As the "all clear" sounded, Violet suddenly realized she didn't have the door key and had dropped the latch. The family returned home, but now Violet was very much aware of that missing footwear as she felt every prickle on her feet.

Violet realized she was locked out, but what could she do? How could she get in? Help was at hand. A man with a ladder came to the rescue, but unfortunately he was too big for the window, and in the darkness Violet, who was terrified of heights, had to squeeze through an upper window to gain access to her home.

I asked Violet to recall what she could about "her" air raid shelter. She remembered the hard seats and the way everyone at first just looked at each other, until group conversations started, which usually lasted the duration of the raid, broken only by the silence that fell when aircraft passed overhead. The silence was often interrupted by the question "are they theirs or ours?" As the sound of the approaching aircraft grew nearer, the "whose" became apparent by the familiar engine noises distinguishing theirs from ours.

One of Violet's children, Peter, found light relief thanks to one of two elderly ladies who shared the shelter. She became so nervous and agitated that she suffered frequently from bad attacks of wind, in all directions. This would trigger off fits of giggles from Peter resulting in a reprimand from mother. However this dear old lady is remembered as having said on one of these occasions, "it's alright, I understand; don't stop him from smiling". This event never ceased to amuse the young Peter.

As time went by, Violet's treks to the shelter ended as numerous households with very young children were provided with "shelter" in their own homes.

This was in the form of a free issue iron table with a protective metal mesh. Violet put a mattress under hers and her children slept within the safety of this construction. Violet and many like her sought refuge under the stairs. Experience had shown that after the raids in Hull, in the houses that were bombed the staircases usually remained intact, thus affording a degree of protection to anyone seeking safety there.

Earlier I mentioned the black-out and its harmful effect on pipe smokers; one such smoker sustained an injury to his pockets during a black-out, for he was caught lighting his pipe as he left the Regal Cinema and this resulted in a £1 fine.

Beverley's Base Hospital (now the Westwood) was to be shared with military personnel and civilian casualties in the event of Air Raids causing injury. The Hospital consisted of eight huts, each holding 42 beds! but was sadly lacking in a vast number of smaller necessities. So at the end of September the W.V.S. held a 'Special Efforts Week' in an attempt to acquire many of those extras. Their shopping list covered practically everything from ash trays to soap dishes, and ward clocks to Hospital linen.

"Beverley" would sail the oceans and help to fight the war, as the result of an ex-US Navy Destroyer being re-named "Beverley". And that wasn't all, for the local branch of the W.V.S. were to adopt the vessel.

Cinema newsreels played a very important part in informing the public of the war activities throughout the world, but probably the most valued items were "our Forces at work", and repeatedly cinemagoers would recognize on the screen a relative at home or abroad. This brought numerous requests, initially to the manager, for a film clip. He in turn referred them to newsreel companies.

One such company did its best to satisfy public requests and actually supplied thousands of enlarged photographs taken from frames of film, many sent back by return of post.

It was known that the enemy intended to use parachute mines, and the first of these fell on Hull on October 22nd at 1.40 a.m. the target being Strathmore Avenue. But before the warning was sounded, two mines had landed causing extensive damage to property, and resulting in many casualties of which two were fatal.

Reporting restrictions forbade the identity of a certain "North-East town" being made known, when at 6.20 p.m. on Sunday October 27th, a German bomber flew over the town, opened fire and machine gunned many of the town's streets. That town was Beverley. Thankfully injuries were restricted to just two men being hit in the feet, but many properties suffered. One house had curtains set on fire by tracer bullets. Numerous shops had their windows broken and people waiting for buses in the Market Place rushed to the safety of nearby shelters for protection. My mother having just alighted from a bus near St. Mary's Church, heard and then saw "a big black bomber" come over and almost touch with North Bar, machine gunning as it went. Thankfully safe, but very shaken, Mother was taken by some soldiers to the NAAFI canteen at Kemps Corner and then escorted home. One bullet was found sometime later lodged in a pew at St. Mary's Church and as a child at Sunday school, I can remember being told of the incident and being shown the damaged pew.

Beryl Brown also recalls the same night, when walking to church with a friend, dressed for the occasion in her one 'good' coat, Beryl brought her friend's attention to a plane flying towards them. The next thing they knew, two Canadian soldiers had dragged them both to the ground. Beryl's first thoughts were for her coat, but soon realized the soldiers' actions were totally honourable and for their protection.

'Flashing' a light wasn't the only offence committed during black-outs, for in October and November four people (and one a lady at that) were found guilty, and fined for committing a nuisance in a public place. It appears they all took certain liberties under the cover of darkness (to be polite, and for family reading — passed water).

As you know, many of the iron railings around properties were requisitioned for war manufacturing industries. However, a few had remained, as a visitor to the town discovered the night he walked into some during a "black-out". Through his accident, he suffered shock and bruising to his ribs, not to mention his broken fountain pen and pencils in his pocket. Someone aware of this occurrence recommended that those railings, like street corners, should be painted white, and so almost nightly the catalogue of "black-out" victims grew.

As a result of the severe bombing of Coventry on November 15th, and difficulties encountered when water supplies failed, questions were asked about Beverley's own water supply in the event of a similar raid. It was thought possible that water might be gained if some of the town's old watercourses were opened up and dammed. Walkergate beck was one such, known to pass under the busiest parts of the town and believed could be an asset in an emergency. Bore holes under the town might also be improved, thus enabling auxiliary pumps access to ample water supplies. These ideas were never adopted and thankfully our town suffered no severe bombings to warrant such drastic measures.

Another Christmas around the corner and no end to the war in sight. The Christmas of 1940 with so many restrictions and of course rationing was reflected only too well in the shops and the absence of well-stocked shelves. But Care's in the Market Place did have a good selection of Caley's Christmas crackers at prices to suit all pockets from 9d to 2/6 a box.

Yet another problem of the war was the risk of diptheria to children. Dr Peter McKinlay, the School Medical Officer, expressed his and the Government's concern at the increased likelihood of the spread of the disease, principally brought about by the war causing a mixing of populations and crowding together in Air Raid shelters. Dr McKinlay urged patients to heed the warning and have their children immunised as quickly as possible.

By the end of the year, Hull hadn't suffered too badly through enemy action, but a dramatic war had been waged on the nerves of the City's population through the constant warnings both day and night.

It is recorded that on one day the sirens sounded six times and on another there were "eight individual warnings". Indeed, the citizens of Hull were suffering through the dangers that awaited in every tomorrow.

*Typical War-time Christmas card.*

# 1941

January 1941 and with it the rationing of clothes; also a new year gift of a bag of sand to every household in the borough!, with instructions that it must be kept dry, and not to let children play with it, as the sand could be valuable when fighting incendiary bomb fires.

Fears of attack from fire bombs were very real and so on January 16th, a demonstration showing ways of dealing with these devices took place. Whilst on film, Ernest Symmons had also covered the subject and it was hoped many members of the public would know what to do, without too much panic or resultant damage.

Still with incendiary raids, and an amusing story from Beryl Brown. On one particular night it had rained heavily, all around was the 'flack' of a raid, and searchlights scoured the night sky for enemy aircraft.

Beryl's father was out on Warden duty, while at home Beryl and her Mum sat listening to the sounds of war around them; but they became curiously attracted to strange sounds coming from the garden.

Carefully they ventured outside and sure enough there was something happening in the garden. Suspecting it to be an incendiary bomb, Beryl rushed into the house to tell her husband, but sleep was more important to him than noises in the garden.

So with no alternative, Beryl and her Mum armed with torch, crept down the garden, ready to run at any second.

The beam of their torch explored the garden, but found no bomb. The sounds continued, then their light caught an intimate moment between Mr & Mrs Hedgehog!

On Wednesday January 29th, a Royal Proclamation decreed that youths aged 18 and 19, along with men 37 to 40 were to register for military service, in order to provide a steady flow of men for the three services.

It could almost have been a dress rehearsal, especially as so much concern had been expressed over the precautions and potential damage that could be expected in an incendiary raid, when around 9.45 p.m. fire was discovered in the Conservative Club in Beverley's North Bar Without. The weather didn't help, with the blizzard wind aggravating the flames. Thankfully two soldiers assisted the caretaker, using stirrup pumps. Also trying to control the fire was the auxiliary fire brigade, until the Town brigade arrived. They encountered problems trying to erect their ladders on the slippery snow and ice that covered the footpath. Then came the difficulty of getting water through the upper windows, but a solution was on hand thanks to Mr. Care 'blowing in' the windows with his 12 bore shotgun! By 2 a.m. the fire was under control, and in appreciation hot tea and cakes were served to the many helpers.

For those not too keen on porridge, then a tempting improvement could be made by the addition of cocoa and/or dried fruits, and if there was any left over, it could be served cold as a fruit fool!

Late February brought fire watching to the fore, and the question of whether it was fair to expect men, many aged 60 and over, to be on duty at midnight, 'watch' through until about 7 a.m., then to go straight off to their work soon after? Surely there must be some younger men somewhere in the town quite capable of doing this duty! Perhaps there were, and some younger people could shortly find themselves fire watchers, as the option was under considera- tion of using older pupils and parents of school children to cover fire watching in the town's schools.

Many Beverley people obviously wanted to take good care of the town's namesake and adopted the Destroyer, HMS Beverley, reflected in the numerous gifts for despatch to the ship's crew. These included, dartboard, football!, 124 knitted comforts, books, games and many more valued items.

March, and the first of those much feared and dreaded raids. It was 8.11 on the night of the 18th when the sirens were heard; half an hour later, chandelier flares hung in the sky making Hull a perfect target. 9.45 p.m. brought the first bomb on an oil extracting factory. Shortly after it was the gas works which were compelled to cease service, then it was the turn of the power station which received an unexploded bomb. Over a hundred high explosive bombs fell during the raid destroying 700 houses beyond use, and starting 700 fires, the resultant death toll being over 90.

The end of March saw the introduction of Preserves Rationing. Jam, marma- lade and treacle were now rationed. On the Beverley Westwood, tractors set to work ploughing up the grassland in the centre of the racecourse, in preparation for growing crops.

The warnings sounded at 8.20 p.m., flares following soon after, but the actual raid didn't start until a few minutes past nine. This was Monday March 31st and a heavy raid to record; in fact not many areas of Hull escaped the bombardment. Buildings fell blocking roads, water mains burst and fires raged everywhere. Of the recorded 200 casualties, 50 were fatal.

It was a sad orange day in 1941 at the Spencer School — for what is an orange day without oranges? This was the first time since 1911 that due to a scarcity of oranges none had been available to give to the children.

Throughout April only minor raids were experienced in Hull, but tragedy struck on the 15th when a parachute bomb fell on a crowded public shelter in Ellis Terrace on Holderness Road, resulting in 200 casualties, 60 people being killed or missing.

Good news for cinemagoers in Hull, especially those wanting film entertain- ment extending to seven days a week, for on April 17th, 25 cinemas had licences granted permitting them to open between 5.30 and 9.30 p.m. each Sunday.

500,000 women who had been born in 1920 were called to register on April 19th. This registration did not mean they would be expected to commence war work immediately; instead it gave some idea of just how many were occupied in useful work and the number available for work of national importance.

Early May and the civilian population was rife with rumours of less petrol being available, due to the increased demands by the three services; but at this stage the matter was still under review. However this did not deter the sale of cars, as Sid Renton advertised a 1940 Austin 8, 2-door saloon De-luxe for only £195.

Once again the generosity of Gordon Armstrong was acknowledged as he gave the nation further money for the purchase of a Spitfire or Hurricane, making this his second in 12 months.

Others were also considering the purchase of bombers for the nation. The Beverley Committee of the National Savings movement, after a meeting in the Mayor's parlour, decided that a week of fund raising should be held with a target of £100,000 set. The dates chosen for the mammoth appeal would be June 14th to 21st. This would be "War Weapons Week" and if all went well could provide five bombers.

£100,000 was a lot of money to raise in peacetime, let alone war; take for example the struggle to raise the £550 to protect the Minster's east window; by May 1941 it still fell a long way short of its target and that collection had been going for months.

The tragedy of blitzed Hull presented a spectacular picture for miles around as the burning city lit up the sky.

The pasture land of Beverley's Westwood proved an ideal vantage point attracting spectators who watched with morbid fascination the City of Hull burning. One "goul" was heard to say "it was a pretty sight". Some people actually travelled many miles to obtain a "good view".

Little did anyone realize during those nights of carnage on May 7th and 8th, 420 people lost their lives, 800 people were injured, 3,000 houses were wrecked or seriously damaged, and 50,000 houses received blast, bomb or shrapnel damage — not a "pretty sight".

Violet Moore remembers that blitz night. When escorting her Mother back home, she saw the transformation of St. John's Street from black-out to what could have been mistaken for daylight as the fires that raged in Hull illuminated the sky and the street. Her vision of the "spectacle" was marred by her thoughts of the tragedy and loss of life that lay behind that scene.

Irene Goodyear from her home in Walkergate also witnessed the sky over Hull ablaze with the Beverley Minster dramatically silhouetted against it.

The sirens sounded at 11.16 p.m. on May 7th, with ten clusters of incendiary bombs heading the raid. Cleveland Street was the first victim of a high explosive bomb at 12.35 a.m. For the next few hours 98 bombs fell in estimated sizes from one to ten hundredweight, along with 28 mines of around twenty hundredweight each.

The following night, the 8th, the raid was more intense. Once again the incendiaries fell first, twelve clusters showing the way for the 190 bombs and 42 mines that followed. Hull was a disaster area, and fires raged throughout the city. The fire brigades battled to deal with around 800 fires and to make matters worse were the vast number of damaged and blocked roads prohibiting access to many burning buildings. King Edward, Jameson and Prospect Streets were all infernos, the fires destroying a great many large stores, hotels, restaurants and numerous small businesses all beyond recognition. Stacks of stored timber on the riverside quay blazed sending sparks into the night sky and starting more fires.

Many thought the raids would never end, but they did; each dawn brought with it the evidence of the enemy's visit. Only in daylight could the full extent of the destruction be realized. A great sadness was felt for the city and its people. Why in war do so many innocents have to die or suffer?

A third night of terror was anticipated when shortly before midnight on the 9th the sirens sounded their threatening cry. But it wasn't to be three in a row as only a few bombs fell at Sutton.

May would be a month never to be forgotten for the majority of Hull's population and thankfully, with the exception of minor raids on the 13th and 29th, the month ended quietly. But June brought further sadness — on the 2nd the fiftieth raid was recorded and although small as such, it had tragic consequences. The 'all clear' had sounded and relieved people were making their way back home from the shelters when the bombs fell. That small raid took the lives of 27 people, all killed in minutes, and in the belief they were safe.


Would you believe it? The Ministry of Agriculture decided the time had come to employ women and pay them £5 per week, plus expenses, to supervise the making of jam, not at jam factories but by the Womens Institutes and other similar bodies. The question was asked, why pay someone to supervise jam-making when all the work is done voluntarily? And surely those involved must have been at it for years and be well aware of the pressure of making ends meet and avoiding waste. So why the expense of a supervisor?

Plans for the Beverley and District War Weapons Week (to be held in June) were well under way by the end of May. The publicity committee had arranged for a cinema van to tour the country areas to announce details of events; the local relay on the radio would also play its part in the campaign, keeping listeners abreast of entertainment and recreation arrangements.

Activities for the week included a procession of the three services, regimental bands, concerts, cricket matches, model aeroplane flying competitions, various regimental displays, dances and much, much more — all designed to entertain and raise that necessary money through war bonds.

Still with money; the administrators of the Poor Children's Boot Fund spent £30-14s-3d on repairing old boots and providing 77 new pairs. And remember that warning earlier about damaging the crops? Well one couple decided to take a short cut through a field of wheat on their cycles. They were caught! The man fined £3 but the woman got off lightly with £1!

Food had been rationed for just 18 months when clothes also came under the umbrella of rationing. From June 1941 the allocation was 66 clothing coupons per person per year, reducing in 1942 to 48! These now became the days of single-breasted jackets for men, with a maximum of three pockets. But it wasn't fashion dictating that men's trousers had to have bottoms no wider than 19 inches and without turnups. It was the Government making these restrictions in an attempt to save cloth. Boys under 12 could only have short trousers!

Men were better off than women, for it was the latter who cared most about what they looked like and missed that 'something new' or different for those special occasions. Make-up and stockings were very difficult to obtain and many resorted to painting their legs with a mixture of face cream and shoe polish, or gravy browning — seams being added with eye-liner pencils and a steady hand.

A nation of needle magicians soon emerged as women worked wonders, turning almost anything into something. Army blankets made good overcoats. Table cloths, curtains, black-out material, parachute silk, in fact any surplus available materials were seen as usable convertible commodities. It was reported that one woman had even made a child's coat from old chamois leathers! The coupon allocation didn't stretch far enough, especially when an adult woman's coat consumed 14 coupons, a pair of shoes 5 and a cardigan 5. A man's coat took 16, a shirt 8, a pullover 5, and shoes 7. So, as will be appreciated, clothes just had to last. To this end the Government produced a series of short propaganda films expounding the necessity for everyone to take care of what they had. On the plus side, many of those specially made clothes under the utility banner, even though economical in their use of cloth, were well designed and manufactured. Many utility items actually became well accepted by the majority of the population and this was mainly attributable to the Government-controlled quality manufacturing system, offering everyone quality items at fixed prices. The manufacturers had to make the best of materials in short supply but this didn't only apply to clothes, for in 1942, due to shortages of timber, only 22 different items of furniture were allowed to be made, again all under the utility banner.


War Weapons Week had been a huge success. The original target of £100,000 had not only been achieved, but more than doubled, reaching £282,378! However, it should be borne in mind that this amount hadn't all come from the public. A high percentage had been given by both local businesses and industry.

The June raids on Hull (with the exception of that tragic June 2nd raid) were, in comparison with the previous month, tolerable, and although the affected areas included Goddard Avenue, East Hull and King George Dock, not forgetting the Stoneferry Bridge, the resultant damage was slight, and mainly to domestic property. Even so, the casualties numbered six of which one was fatal.


On June 22nd Germany invaded Russia. So much for their treaty, again nothing more than a scrap of paper to them.

# Farmers-
## —they rely on you!

We're all in it together. Even children have to take the risks of war and you cannot guarantee their safety. You can provide their food. Top-dress corn and grassland, and **grow more food with**

# SULPHATE of AMMONIA

*Dig for victory with sulphate of ammonia. Advertisement from Beverley Guardian, 8th March 1941.*

*Public Notice on meat shortages, Beverley Guardian, January 1941.*

OWING to the shortage of all classes of Meat, the BEVERLEY AND RURAL DISTRICT MEAT BUYING GROUP will be compelled to CLOSE THEIR SHOPS AND VANS for the sale of Meat on MONDAYS and TUESDAYS, commencing JANUARY 6th, 1941, UNTIL FURTHER NOTICE

*The result of an incendiary bomb in Hull's King Edward Street/Prospect Street area, 4th April 1941. Photo by courtesy of City of Hull Record Office.*

*An unexploded bomb at the Gipsyville allotments, Hull, on 9th April 1941. Photo by courtesy of City of Hull Record Office.*

*"Blitzed"* – *the Prospect Street/Paragon Street bus garage, Hull, following the raid on 8th May 1941. Photo by courtesy of City of Hull Record Office.*

*Skeleton of a mill, pictured from the River Hull, 14th May 1941. Photo by courtesy of City of Hull Record Office.*

*Support the Forces' "Comforts Fund", from the Beverley Guardian, 31st May 1941.*

*"War Weapons Week" in Beverley, June 1941. Advertisement from the Beverley Guardian.*

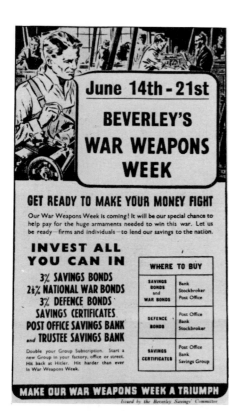

*"War Weapons Week" in Beverley, June 1941. Advertisement from the Beverley Guardian.*

*Frame enlargement from film taken by Ernest Symmons during Beverley's "War Weapons Week", June 1941.*

*Frame enlargement from film taken by Ernest Symmons during Beverley's "War Weapons Week", June 1941.*

*"Road Up". Hull's Kingston Street/Commercial Road, 16th July 1941. Photo by courtesy of City of Hull Record Office.*

*"Spitfire Week" celebrations, as announced in the Beverley Guardian.*

*War Savings Campaign, from the Beverley Guardian, 12th July 1941.*

*Mayor Watts pictured during "Spitfire Week", August 1941. Frame enlargement from film taken by Ernest Symmons.*

*Children covering a "Spitfire" with pennies during Beverley's "Spitfire Week". Frame enlargement from film taken by Ernest Symmons.*

*"We Want Spitfires". Frame enlargement from film taken by Ernest Symmons, August 1941.*

# WARNING!

## Any person

## BURNING OR DESTROYING WASTEPAPER

(WRAPPING PAPER, CARDBOARD BOXES, ENVELOPES, NEWSPAPERS, MAGAZINES, Etc.)

## IS GUILTY OF AN OFFENCE AGAINST THE NATIONAL WAR EFFORT

Every scrap is needed for essential
national requirements.

Save it for local Council collections.

*Encouragement to "save paper" for the war effort, September 1941.*

*Christmas celebrations, 1941, as depicted in the Beverley Guardian.*

64

*Encouragement to "save paper" for the war effort, September 1941.*

*Christmas celebrations, 1941, as depicted in the Beverley Guardian.*

War Weapons Week was over but not forgotten, for the week's events had been faithfully captured on film by the cinema proprietor, Ernest Symmons, for his ever popular weekly Playhouse News.

It was good news for the jam makers. The Food Ministry announced that during the month of July the sugar ration would be doubled, thus allowing 2lbs of sugar on each ration book. Generosity in another form came from the Mayor of Beverley Massachusetts USA to Beverley's Mayor with a donation of £378-10s-2 credited through the bank to the Mayoress's Spitfire Fund.

If you hadn't already dug all your garden or allotment up for growing essential foods, and you still had a stretch spare, then the Ministry of Agriculture would be pleased to know and offer help if you could breed a few rabbits. The idea was to form rabbit clubs whereby members prepared to produce rabbits for food would be allowed rations of bran. However, not less than 50% of the meat and fur produced had to be sold to the "common food pool", retailers, canteens, restaurants, or any other interested parties.

From the relative calm of June to a disastrous July, with the first bad raid on the 11th, when the Central and South Western areas of Hull were attacked. Out of almost 150 casualties 21 proved fatal. A few days later, on the 15th, a raid of similar proportions on the North West side of the City brought the death toll to 25 and left over 50 people injured.

The last heavy raid of the month came on the 18th, resulting in direct hits on the Rank Flour Mill, the East Hull Gasworks and the Reckitts Factory. This raid caused 140 deaths, 108 casualties, and damage to almost 7,000 houses, 1,500 of which were uninhabitable.

As the summer of '41 wore on, so the use of the car came under threat, as it was announced that there would be a 50% cut in the supplementary petrol allowances. This news affected many and within a few weeks would result in many cars being "laid-up".

Wednesday, August 6th, brought their Majesties the King and Queen on an informal visit to Hull, and although the news of their visit had been kept quiet, crowds lined the streets to welcome the Royal visitors.

During their visit the King and Queen were taken to see some of the worst affected areas resulting from those nights of the blitz a few months earlier. What footpaths remained were packed tight with loyal well-wishers and everywhere on piles of rubble and debris the citizens of Hull stood, waving, cheering and shouting their welcome greetings to the Royal visitors. But it wasn't just the bomb-damaged City on display — its people were. So many of them affected by the War; the bereaved, the homeless. Those people presented themselves in great numbers along the Royal route. Not all could meet the Royal couple, but many of those citizens within the voluntary and paid services were present and were acknowledged for their bravery and stamina during difficult times.

Another call was made for money on August 16th with the opening of Spitfire Week. The fund sponsored by the Mayoress had already reached £2,000 but much more was needed to buy that plane, and so the good people of

Beverley were once again invited to give and support.

The week was opened with a Civic Ceremony at the Market Cross, and thanks to the East Yorkshire Regimental Band, Spitfire Week got off to a rousing start.

Many events had been pre-planned, from a concert on the 17th at the Marble Arch Cinema to outdoor dancing at the Norwood Cricket Ground (sadly the boxing match had to be cancelled due to the contestants being 'posted' to the South of England).

On August 17th the Germans took Kiev.

The August 18th raid on Central and East Hull resulted in three shelters being damaged and 20 people losing their lives.

On Tuesday, August 26th, HRH the Princess Royal came to Beverley, although the visit lasted only about half an hour. The Princess was shown the W.V.S. work rooms, where she spoke with many of the helpers, acknowledging their voluntary work for the war effort.

Over a thousand houses in South West, Central and East Hull became victims of the August 31st raid and 44 more lives were lost. Thankfully some good news came to please the many supporters of the Mayoress's Spitfire Fund, for by September 13th it had reached £3,563-13-1.

Once again concern was expressed over the town's water supply and sufficient quantities being available to fight fires in the event of heavy raids. This time the suggestion was not as earlier of damming the old Beverley watercourses, but the supply or construction of large tanks on spare land throughout the town. These tanks did materialise and although principally used for their intended purpose of water-storage, they also became receptacles for all sorts of rubbish!

On September 21st the Priory Sidings on Hessle Road were singled out for attack, resulting in four railway tracks being damaged.

Good news for cheese lovers. Thanks to improved supplies, cheese would be available to more catering establishments than it had been previously. This would in effect enable public houses serving meals now to allow one tenth of an ounce per customer. Any such hostelry serving forty meals a day would qualify for a weekly allowance of $1\frac{3}{4}$lbs!

Although still short of its target, the Minster East Window Preservation Fund had, by early October, reached £400.

On October 19th came the announcement by Stalin that Moscow was in a state of seige.

November 12th and the 'Paper Order' came into force. This was a very necessary attempt to save paper; from that date nothing other than food could be wrapped in it, and the use of advertising handbills and posters was strictly controlled.

It was thought that the numerous Government departments should set an example and reduce some of their forms from triplicate to duplicate. Nevertheless, Greens in the Saturday Market advertised that they had no shortage of domestic stationery and held stocks of everything from shelf lining paper to sandwich flags. But what when stocks ran out? The order prohibited the future production of Christmas and other greetings cards as well as table stationery. Additional restrictions were soon to follow and these would affect calendar production.

"Music for the Soldiers" was another public appeal when the public were asked to help in supplying portable cabinet gramophones of the non-electrical variety. Already a record library had been established but there was a desperate shortage of gramophones. Their acquisition would enable musical comforts to be provided for the thousands of music loving soldiers serving in isolated searchlight posts.

The issue of Sunday cinema opening had been under discussion for some time, not so much for the public but for forces personnel as so many of them could be seen wandering the streets on Sundays. It was felt entertainment should be provided. The Secretary of State had authorised Councils to grant licences to interested parties. In Beverley, however, the Council said "No" to Sunday cinemas (strange to think — no Sunday cinema but all three Beverley cinemas held performances on Christmas Day!).

December 8th brought the declaration of war on Japan by Britain and the United States. A few days later, on the 11th, Germany declared war on the United States.

The war brought many changes, in particular a role for women away from the home and family through their involvement in the war effort. It had happened during the first war and repeated itself during the second, but this time it had a lingering effect. Many women found they enjoyed the freedom away from the kitchen sink, nappies and other domestic chores, thus founding the Working Woman.

Before the war only one in three women had jobs and the majority of those were employed in domestic services. However conscription took the men away, leaving behind 2 million vacancies to be filled. With the expanding war industry the only solution was the now-necessary employment of women.

The call to arms was also seized upon by many women who felt the desire to wear a uniform and be trained as military personnel. Three months into the war, 43,000 women had become members of the A.T.S. (Auxiliary Territorial Service).

Many were tempted by the glamour surrounding the A.T.S: the prospects of travel abroad, the opportunity of meeting new and interesting people, plus of course an anticipated fulfilment of the ambition to do many things to serve one's country that it was believed only men could do. In reality conditions were often hard and difficult, not to mention the overlooked aspect of discipline — and many were totally disenchanted.

There were a great number of women who did join the Armed Services and accepted discipline as part of their training not only for established roles in catering and offices, but more skilled and technical duties relating to the defence of the country.

However, on December 18th compulsory conscription was announced of women aged between 20 and 30. In theory they had a choice of Civil Defence, the Land Army, the Services or factory work, but in reality it was the Army or factories.

Cinemas open Christmas Day, and Banks open Boxing Day! 1941 would go on record as having no Boxing Day for it was cancelled. Even so, Christmas came and once again during that time of family togetherness many felt a deep sadness seeing those empty chairs, in some homes maybe for the second Christmas in succession.

The black-out brought little cheer, as did the Christmas fare with less poultry, less rich Christmas puds and little if any icing on the cakes. And if the recent paper restrictions hadn't affected your Christmas card receipts, then you were urged to send them for salvage.

# 1942

The year started with yet another appeal for an alternative water supply to that from the mains, due to the serious shortage of water that resulted each night when the supply was cut off. You can well imagine the problems facing the fire department having to find water before they could fight a fire. This had been the difficulty a few days earlier on Boxing Night when a fire had started in the premises of a Timber Merchant in Lairgate. Twenty minutes had elapsed before any water could be brought to play on the fire. Making matters even worse, when water was available the pressure was insufficient to keep the fire engine pumping to its full capacity and when another engine used the same main, then the already poor 170 gallons a minute dropped to 120! Relief was expressed that this particular fire hadn't happened in a more built up area, for had it been, then the damage to property could have been disastrous.

Still with liquids and bad news for drinkers. Exports to Britain of that popular Irish stout, Guinness, were reduced, and due to labour shortages in the brewing industry, along with attempts to conserve malt, the Ministry of Food decided to reduce the average gravity of beer by 5 per cent.

Paper was still needed for salvage resulting in an appeal to builders, painters and decorators to hand over their old and hefty wallpaper books. Their weight and volume alone could make a healthy contribution to the campaign.

In an effort to save clothing coupons men were advised to stitch a strip of narrow black velvet ribbon along the inside of their trousers to reduce the friction caused between shoe and trouser, thus minimising wear. The advice to women when acquiring silk stockings was to dip them in methylated spirits —even though the toes and heels might wear out at least with this treatment they wouldn't ladder!

By mid February plans were well under way again for the extraction of monies from the people of Beverley and District. This time the target was £120,000, the cost of a Corvette warship, and as with previous fund-raising events "Warship Week" would be no exception.

It doesn't seem to be many pages ago since we heard that the need for public shelters was a focal point for discussion and concern. Well, I was pleased to find details of just what was available in Beverley in the way of shelter protection. By the end of February there were 26 public shelters, and for those houses that were not adequately protected (of which there were 643) there were a further 167 communal shelters.

Four shelters had been provided for schools and somewhere in the region of 100 requests had been made for Morrison Table Shelters.

Apparently a town of Beverley's size and category was required to provide shelter for only one fifth of its population, but thanks to the efforts of the Civil Defence Committee, shelter was provided for about half the town's residents.

March 7th brought news of the Japanese landing in New Guinea, and the evacuation of Rangoon by the British Burmese Army. Beverley's Warship Week officially started the same day with a launching from the Market Cross of a model Corvette followed by the actual ceremony taking place in the Regal Ballroom. During the week that followed musical entertainment was provided daily by the band of the East Yorkshire Regiment. There were also dances, whist drives and a concert at the Marble Arch Cinema, Midnight Matinee at the Playhouse, plus a great many other events all designed to gently and pleasurably encourage wallets and purses to open in support of the war effort.

The response was incredible, the total reaching £302,710 and representing a donation of £9-6s-8 per head of population; but of course the bulk of the figure had been raised thanks to numerous substantial investments from businesses ranging from £100 to £10,000.

Since the introduction of soap rationing, the public was urged to take more care of their skin. Well-known brand manufacturers faced serious restrictions in the amount of raw materials available; this in turn created a shortage of numerous cosmetic items forcing many towards the 'black market'. There existed products of inferior and suspicious quality that were known to cause a variety of skin problems.

The black market had become very lucrative business, due in part to some people not wanting their full ration quota. This meant that certain commodities were available to established customers, but for a price; in other words if you had the money and coupons it was then possible to purchase that bit extra of those hard-to-come-by, and luxury items: butter, sugar, tea, and so the list went on. But this 'under the counter' bartering was only the tip of the black market iceberg, as bigger things were happening all over the country with everything from stockings, meat and petrol to ration books. In fact you name it, and it could be traced to the 'market', which often left the business fraternity moving into organised crime, resulting in frequent professional thefts.

Although not revealed until after the war the largest black market theft had been that of around 100,000 new ration books, each with a street value of £5. This represented £500,000 of black market currency in circulation, which by today's values amounts to around £20 million! And that's a lot of money to lose.

Here is an example from those days of rationing and the flexibility, that existed to the mutual benefit of all parties.

Young Peter was experiencing pre-birthday excitement; his mother prepared a small birthday tea for him and a couple of his school friends. But little did she know, as she made a few potted meat sandwiches with a jelly and custard dessert, that Peter had invited almost all his classmates. Fourteen would be arriving for tea!

Mother was panic-stricken and angry. What food she had could not feed all those mouths, but she didn't want to refuse the excited youngster. So hastily she went to a nearby grocer's shop where she was known. Explaining the circumstances she appealed for help to feed the unexpected guests by borrowing from the next week's coupons! Help was at hand for the friendly grocer provided from 'under the counter' and 'round the back' bread, potted meat and marga-rine. The appreciative mum left with profuse thanks. But that jelly and custard still had to go round ..... and it did!

The first three months of 1942 thankfully were free from raids and afforded a welcome opportunity to repair buildings and clean up. At the same time newcomers to the services were being trained, replacing those taken through National Service. But those glorious weeks of quiet came to an end when the new season of raids opened on April 13th, with West Hull being the target.

Another cut in the petrol ration forced even more motorists off the road for the Easter of 1942. Not only did the motorist save petrol, but wear and tear on tyres too, and the public were discouraged from travelling by train, as needless journeys handicapped the movement of vital war traffic. In essence Easter should be spent within walking or cycling distance of home, or as a better and more productive alternative one was encouraged to 'dig for victory'.

With the basic ration of petrol being reduced by half during the months of April, May and June the Secretary of Petroleum suggested that even more cars should be taken off the roads, especially those that were not genuinely needed to benefit the war effort or the community direct.

News to delight many youngsters came with the proposal that the Army Cadet Force should be expanded nationally providing boys between the ages of 14 and 17 with pre-military service training. Probably it was the spirit of wartime adventure that attracted so many young recruits and the chance to wear with pride the forces' new uniform — khaki battledress. But this was a force designed to teach the youngsters not just the "rules of conduct in life" but invaluable military training which would of course be an asset when later joining the Regular Army. However, there was just one minor snag, for although the uniform was free, the boots were not.

Good news for those employed in shipbuilding and engineering. The Board of Trade decided to allow supplementary clothing coupons, 30 extra for tank and bilge cleaners, 25 to those in shipyards whose work involved acetylene welding, burners, boiler cleaners and scalers. The remaining workers in these industries would qualify for 10 and 15 extra coupons only.

May 8th and Germany began preliminary offensives against the Soviet Union.

I wonder what the feeling amongst school children was when told that Local Education By-Laws had been overridden by Defence Regulations. In plain language, it effectively meant that children of 12 and over were exempt from compulsory school attendances, but the enforced holiday was only to allow them to help meet the seasonal needs of agriculture. However, the exemptions had not to exceed 20 absences from school in a year except in emergencies. Children under 14 could only be employed for half days, and for the other half they had to attend school.

*Save water for fighting fires,
January 1942.*

THE SIGNAL IS SAVE

for
**YOUR WARSHIP WEEK**

The Navy has signalled "ACTION." Day and night our ships plough the seas — seeking out and destroying the enemy. There's a signal for you, too — that signal is SAVE! Make your Warship Week a smash hit by investing for all you're worth in War Savings.

Go to a Post Office or your Bank or Stockbroker and invest your money in 3% Savings Bonds 1955-65, 2½% National War Bonds 1949-51, 3% Defence Bonds, or Savings Certificates, or deposit your savings in the Post Office or Trustee Savings Bank. Buy Savings Stamps at 6d and 2/6d each from a Post Office, Trustee Savings Bank, or your Savings Group.

**INVEST ALL YOU CAN IN**

3% Savings Bonds

2½% National War Bonds

3% Defence Bonds

Savings Certificates

Post Office Savings Bank

Trustee Savings Bank

March 7th — 14th
**BEVERLEY & DISTRICT**
OBJECTIVE £110,000
Cost of a Corvette

## PLAYHOUSE

TELEPHONE NO. 15

BEVERLEY & DISTRICT
### WARSHIP WEEK

MARCH 7th—14th.

*Cancel possible defeat...*
*Ships our Lifeline.*

Ships, and more ships, are needed for food and munitions. Warships, and more warships, are required to fight a daring and ruthless foe. Make no mistake—our existence is threatened.

**YOU CAN HELP THE NATION BY INVESTING YOUR MONEY IN WAR SAVINGS CERTIFICATES AND GOVERNMENT BONDS**

MONDAY, FEBRUARY 23rd—3 days          MATINEE—Sunday at 3-0
JUDITH ANDERSON · DENNIS O'KEEFE in
**LADY SCARFACE**
Drama.
Also Guy Kibbee in " SCATTERGOOD BAINES "—Comedy Drama

THURSDAY, FEBRUARY 26th—3 days only          MATINEE—Thursday at 2-30
GEORGE MURPHY · LUCILLE BALL in
**THE NAVY STEPS OUT**
Forget your troubles, and see the season's greatest laugh show !   Produced by Harold Lloyd.

*Beverley and "Warship Week", 7th to 14th March 1942.*

*Interior of communal sleeping-shelter, Fifth Avenue School, Hull, June 1942.*
*Photo by courtesy of City of Hull Record Office.*

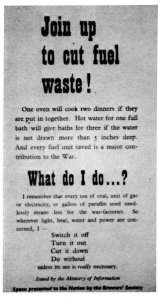

## Join up to cut fuel waste!

One oven will cook two dinners if they are put in together. Hot water for one full bath will give baths for three if the water is not drawn more than 5 inches deep. And every fuel unit saved is a major contribution to the War.

### What do I do...?

I remember that every ton of coal, unit of gas or electricity, or gallon of paraffin used needlessly means less for the war-factories. So wherever light, heat, water and power are concerned, I —

    Switch it off
    Turn it out
    Cut it down
    Do without
    unless its use is *really* necessary.

*Issued by the Ministry of Information*
Space presented to the Nation by the Brewers' Society

*Saving power, October 1942.*

## POPPY DAY
### 1942

As a wartime economy measure, and owing to the restriction of materials used in the making of poppies, the supply of the larger types (1/- & 2/6) is very limited.

The Local Appeal Organiser earnestly requests the public for their kind indulgence and most generous support by accepting the *smaller* emblems if the larger ones are not available.

*Economies in poppies, Armistice Day 1942.*

*"Hospital Helps"*
*for Beverley's*
*Westwood Hospital,*
*under the care of*
*Miss Whiting,*
*Summer 1942.*

What is believed to be the biggest bomb dropped on Hull made its mark on May 19th in Scarborough Street, resulting in 200 casualties, 50 proving fatal. Damage to property could not be accurately assessed due to the bomb flattening a great many buildings over a vast area.

We all know our reaction when someone says "Would you like to see my holiday photos?" How many dare say no? And so out of politeness the photos are usually passed around to favourable comments, but did you know that in 1942 the Admiralty actually appealed for holiday photos to help in the military offensives? What they wanted was any photographs of other countries depicting roads, railways, bridges, harbours, power stations, oil installations etc; in fact anything that could help them build a better overall picture of the world outside Great Britain.

May 30th put Cologne on the receiving end of the RAF's 1,000 bomber raid.

All that trouble taken to get those public shelters and now there were complaints of some being in a poor state. One on the Mill Lane estate had bricks and sandbags strewn all over the place; it was felt that this damage could be attributed to children who found great delight playing in the shelters. Councillors aware of the situation thought the Mill lane shelter was an isolated case as an inspection of others had found them quite satisfactory.

During the 1914-18 war there had been 16,000 registered conscientious objectors, but for this war the figure had risen dramatically to 64,000. Eyebrows were raised in certain circles and the question asked why so many objectors now? Was there an organisation somewhere encouraging objectors, possibly one of Hitler's Fifth Columns? Some thought the so called pacifist groups and the origin of their finances merited a closer look.

At last those iron railings would have to go in the interests of the war effort. The Ministry of Works and Planning stated that, commencing on Monday July 20th, all railings had to be removed. It was felt this would be the end of an era as many of the railings had been erected before the first war and the high cost of replacing them after this war could prove prohibitive to a number of households (to this day there are still many walls in the town that exhibit the remains of the iron railing removal).

For the second time in 1942 the citizens of Hull were permitted a break from the raids, athough they were never allowed to escape the strain and anxiety that came with each sounding of the sirens. With the exception of an overnight raid on August 1st, Hull was able to rest reasonably peacefully again until October.

Most times when in my researches I found reference to a North East town I invariably thought of Hull. The censor and Ministry of Air didn't want the enemy to know where their bombs had fallen, so when I saw the headline "Raider dropped bombs on a North East town" in the August 8th edition of the Beverley Guardian, my immediate reaction was of Hull. That is until I checked the record of bombs dropped on the city, and found nothing listed for that day. Then as I started reading about the incident, certain details triggered my memory, and I recalled some things I had been told years ago. This was a report of the raid on Beverley, and the bombs dropped in Flemingate, also of how old Mother Riley had been responsible for saving a great many lives. Apparently a "stick" of bombs was dropped by a single enemy aircraft on what is thought to have been a "tip-and-run" raid, the bombs falling in Flemingate. One person, a Mrs Snowden, lost her life as a direct result of the raid, but the final death toll reached three when a soldier, Stanley Lawrence, died of injuries caused by the explosion as he cycled along Flemingate at the fatal time. The third person was Charlie Cross, who was feeding his rabbits when the tragedy struck. Many people living in the area had minor injuries from flying glass and a number suffered as a result of shock.

Ted Wilson escaped with only a black eye. He was out feeding his pigs at the time. They were all buried, but were found to be alive when dug out later. Damage to property was extensive, 30 houses needing major repairs whilst a further 80 required minor work.

And just how was "Old Mother Riley" credited with saving lives? Well, the film "Old Mother Riley M.P." was showing at the Marble Arch cinema, and thankfully the afternoon matinee had attracted many people from the Flemingate area, especially children. One fact was certain: had there not been that matinee the casualty list would have been much longer.

That afternoon is vividly recalled by Violet Moore who, taking advantage of good drying weather, was hanging out her baby's nappies, when she suddenly heard the recognisable sound of an enemy aircraft approaching. On looking up she saw one fly over very low. Moments later there was a "terrific bang" causing soot to fall down her chimney and the doors to slam. Some people rushed from the street into her house to seek shelter. Then panic struck as Violet realized that her two children had been playing outside. Hastily she pushed past those in the way and then saw, much to her relief, a man escorting her children home. Apparently he had just arrived in time to stop young Peter from picking up a piece of red hot shrapnel. It was then apparent to all that the aircraft seen overhead moments earlier had dropped a bomb nearby.

I talked with Arthur James about the Flemingate raid and from him discovered that four bombs fell in the area. Arthur was eleven or twelve at the time and from his vantage point in Riding Fields Square actually saw the bombs leave the aircraft. He and some friends had gone out to play after the 'all clear' had sounded, when they heard and saw the plane pass overhead. Immediately after seeing the deadly package fall, Arthur and company wasted no time in going to investigate, but on arrival were prohibited from going too close. However, they soon realized the seriousness of the situation; the stables at Hodgson's Tannery had received a direct hit, resulting in the death of a horse, (that I didn't know, but was of course aware of the other fatalities).

Arthur went on to tell of the bomb that fell one night on Greenwood Avenue, thankfully with no resultant loss of life although numerous properties nearby did suffer substantial damage.

As our chat continued I was to learn of other wartime happenings; about the parachute mines that fell in an area west of the Army Barracks on Victoria Road, and the spitfire accidentally shot down and crash landing in a field near Woodmansey. Arthur had seen this happen from his bedroom window. The plane was first picked out by the searchlight, then the guns opened fire. Seconds later flames were seen and down it went. Believing it to be the enemy the spectators raised a cheer; unfortunately the pilot had omitted to display his identity lights! But the story doesn't end there for that pilot was a Pole unable to speak a word of English, and when he was approached by the Home Guard they thought he was the enemy!

As well as Beverley receiving its first tragic bombing raid in August, the month also saw the introduction of compulsory fire-guard orders for women aged between 20 and 45. This effectively established women in the role of fire watchers. However, only when all eligible men had been utilised would they become active.

On August 22nd it was announced that Brazil had declared war on Germany and Italy.

On a 'sweeter' note, from August 24th the weekly sweet ration was increased to 4 ounces per person, but only for a limited period of eight weeks. Thereafter it was anticipated that it would be reduced to 3 ounces.

Did you know that dogs were 'called-up' for war service? but on a voluntary basis! Roles included patrol, sentry, reconnaissance and guard duty at war factories. Heading the list was the alsatian, followed closely by cross breeds, but only where one or both parents were of a specific breed; then came the collie, performing best as messengers. Of course the dogs were only loaned for the duration of the war, and remember it was 'voluntary' service!

Reynolds at the corner of Railway Street had on offer "Re-conditioned Battle Dress Uniforms" available in all sizes at only 21/- and no coupons necessary. However, their sale was strictly to agricultural workers.

Sunday November 15th was Civil Defence Day throughout the country. It was a day of remembrance, and acknowledgement of our victory in Egypt along with the defeat of German air attacks. The Prime Minister, Winston Churchill, decreed that church bells throughout the country could be rung for the first time since June 1940, when they were only to be sounded as a warning of invasion. But on this occasion their sounds were of celebration.

From joy, to sadness in Hull. On December 20th tragedy struck — the sirens sounded too late, the bombs had been dropped and lives lost.

As the fourth Christmas of war drew closer the main topic for concern wasn't so much the shortage of traditional festive fare, but of water. Owing to a lower rainfall, supplies were getting desperate. Beverley's water supply was now cut off each night from 7 pm to 7 am, but this restriction did little to ease the situation and additional measures were needed; the water would have to be cut off from 2 pm to 4 pm each day in the hope that this would help. Even the top-up supply of 200,000 gallons daily from Richard Hodgson could not be maintained due to their own increased demand and the well levels having now fallen. Two schemes were under consideration, but in the meantime the only water available during the night was that left in the mains at the lower end of the town. Therefore, if householders in that area selfishly used it, the mains would be left dry, which in the event of fires could have disastrous consequences.

Jessie Oston's Uncle Frederick farmed land in Figham, which is slightly south east of Beverley. Jessie and her mother went to live with uncle on his farm and it's from that area that her wartime memories originate, now retold in her own words.

"Apart from remembering the wonderful spirit which prevailed during those years of war, when everyone seemed to help everyone else, I often compare that time with the present, when we live in a world of unnecessary violence. I worked at the Midland Bank from 1941-1945, and at Balance Time we often left very late at night. The streets were pitch black. I had to walk alone out to the farm, carrying a tiny torch, half-blacked out, yet never once did I have any reason to feel afraid. The only dangerous incident was on one of those nights, when walking along the drive to the farm from the gatehouse, I suddenly heard deep breathing and was aware of 'someting' in my path. I soon discovered a number of horses lying down asleep on the drive. It could have been nasty if I had walked into them. I turned back to the gatehouse and told Roy Walker, the neatherd, and he came with me. After that night, that good friend insisted on seeing me across, no matter what the time was — just another example of the way people helped each other.

Bread wasn't rationed until the war ended. When my husband returned in October 1945 after being a P.O.W. in Japanese hands, we bought bread at a shop in Beckside belonging to Mr. & Mrs. Mayes. People (some whom we didn't know) would leave their unused coupons so that we could get extra bread to feed him up!"

From one act of wartime kindness to another. It was a special Christmas present for about 100 children, all of them belonging to Beverley prisoners of war. The treat was organised by courtesy of Ernest Symmons when he invitd the children to the Playhouse Cinema to see the Walt Disney film "Dumbo". This was followed by tea at the Rambla cafe, kindly provided by Mr. Stephenson who also gave each child half-a-crown, a welcome if small substitute for those missing fathers held in enemy hands.

# 1943

The first raid on Hull in the new year was like the last of 1942; the year was but three days old when again warning sirens sounded too late and the bombs came first.

1943 brought with it a solution to Beverley's water shortage. Agreement had been reached between the Borough Council and Hull Corporation, who promised to supply additional water to the town at the cost of installing the necessary main plus 8d per 1,000 gallons. This would help to alleviate the long periods when the water was cut off.

The January 15th raid meant work for the Gas Indentification Service when phosphorous bombs were dropped on Hull. However, this raid was to be the last for five incredible bomb free months.

On February 22nd H.R.H. The Princess Royal visited Beverley. Her tour included an inspection of the W.V.S. East Riding County Clothing store in Newbegin. After inspecting the enormous stocks of clothes available for evacuees, and speaking to the many people involved in the work and organisation of the W.V.S., her Royal Highness then went on to County Hall where at the end of her visit she was served with tea.

Good news for those townspeople who had prior to the war relied on church clock chimes, for as from Monday March 22nd both the Beverley Minster and St Mary's Church would be allowed to have their chimes restored, but only during daylight hours.

From timekeeping to charity, and kind thoughts for a colleague who had been disabled as a result of having lost a leg. The shipyard platoon of the Home Guard organised a dance in his honour at Hodgson's Ballroom and the evening was a huge success, raising over £20 for this good cause.

Members of the No.3 Division of the Beverley Civil Defence Wardens and Messenger Services announced that they would like to provide a reproduction peal of bells for St Nicholas Church in Holme Church Lane. This would involve a recording of pealing bells being made and a loudspeaker placed in the church tower to play them back! It was felt this would be a permanent memorial of their efforts. Their suggestion was put before the Parochial Church Council, who unanimously agreed that the offer should be accepted (I wonder how many readers will remember those reproduction bells on record and their sounds as they called worshippers to church).

Sad news hit Beverley during May when it was disclosed that the town's adopted destroyer, H.M.S. Beverley, had fought its last battle whilst on active service in the North Atlantic. Regrettably though, due to restrictions imposed by the censor, no further details of this tragedy were made available. However it was hoped that another vessel might at some time in the future be adopted by the town.

Wings for Victory Week officially started on Saturday May 29th at 2.30 p.m. although the Band of the East Yorkshire Regiment had played for an hour previously. Perhaps it was the music that had helped to attract the crowds who turned out in their hundreds and contributed to the wonderful carnival atmosphere.

As on previous occasions the cry was out for money, with a target figure of £200,000. In Beverley the entertainment and activities ranged from a wartime food exhibition to speeches by school children and a great many dances.

Out at Cherry Burton their opening ceremony was followed by a demonstration by the Army Physical Training instructors. The auction of a ewe and lamb raised £850, a bottle of rum £100, and Cherry Burton grown strawberries must have been special as a pound of them went for £81! In total the sale raised £4,000-2s-6d. All credit to the people of Beverley and district, as their efforts and commitment to the savings movement realized £383,965.

More appreciation of the fund raising by the Civil Defence Wardens and Messengers. At last that reproduction peal of bells for St Nicholas Church had become a reality when on Sunday June 20th a service of dedication was held.

As you may remember, throughout the darker days of the war Hull was never mentioned by name, only as a "North East Town", or occasionally "a town on the East Coast". This changed after a raid in June when for the first time Hull was named in the reports.

The June 24th attack was somewhat different. It was the first raid on Hull in which anti-personnel or Butterfly Bombs were dropped, small enough to lodge in the smallest crevices and harnessing a great destructive power if handled or disturbed. Their coming was anticipated and the public had been prepared for their arrival.

From Butterfly Bombs to a road accident, thankfully with no serious injury or loss of life. A party of school children travelling into the country for pea picking had a lucky escape when their bus was in collision with an army vehicle, near Bishop Burton. The bus was turned completely over but fortunately many of the children managed to get out through broken windows. Nine of the boys were taken to, and detained in, the Beverley Emergency Hospital for treatment of cuts to their hands and scalps.

Would you believe it? Here we are in the middle of a war and there are people discussing the possibility of constructing a tunnel under the River Humber!

It's that problem with the water again. Even with improved supplies there was in certain circles deep concern over the authorities still cutting off water supplies each night. There was also fear about the half hour lost as the mains filled again. This was not much good in an emergency, and it was asked if the water could be turned off in different districts, instead of everywhere at once, thus retaining water in a good many mains.

From water to milk, and with all the shortages created throughout the war there must have been many people delighted to hear the news that the price of milk was coming down again, to just 4d. a pint.

The last heavy raid on Hull came on July 14th when the enemy delivered great quantities of high explosive and phosphorous bombs, plus of course incendiaries in generous helpings, many being explosive. Loss of life and casualties were extensive as was the damage to property. There were serious disruptions when a road over a railway bridge was destroyed, causing chaos to both road and rail traffic.

The enemy action on York in 1942 had resulted in the City's Guildhall being extensively damaged. With discussions for rebuilding in hand, Beverley's Mayor, Councillor A. Watts, suggested that one of the Westwood oak trees could possibly be incorporated in the new building. It was a grand idea and given full support by the pasture masters.

August 4th saw the commencement of Book Fortnight. This was a campaign held throughout Yorkshire to obtain books, not only for salvage, but to supply the forces and the many blitzed libraries. Beverley's target was to collect 25,000 books, with two of the town's cinemas participating; the Playhouse and Marble Arch organised children's matinees where admission was only gained by books, five books qualified for a 10d. or 1/- seat, but for ten books or more access to the 1/9 or 2/3 seats was possible. For the Playhouse matinee children queued for an hour, stretching round almost as far as the Market Cross. This resulted in 7,200 books being collected, and down the road at the Marble Arch their collection reached 2,000 (I felt the Playhouse success may have been attributable to the film screened. They showed "The Arabian Nights" while at the Marble Arch it was "A Ministry of Information Film Show for Children". Even so almost 10,000 books in two collections was a very praiseworthy effort).

The outcome of this book campaign was a surprise to many, especially when it was announced that the target of 25,000 had been more than doubled, achieving a magnificent collection amounting to 50,250.

As I'm sure you must have realized, throughout these years cinema was the major entertainment of the population. Audience figures before the war were high at 20 million a week, but the war brought record weekly attendances of an incredible 32 million! Going to the pictures wasn't expensive, as for a few shillings one could escape from that drab austere world outside and for at least a couple of hours revel in comfort, luxury and the glamour that only those Picture Palaces could provide.

The majority of programmes offered exceptional value for money with a 'B' feature or a support film in black and white. This invariably whetted the appetite for the big picture which, besides boasting its stars, was "Color by Technicolor". But the night out wasn't complete without the ever popular cartoon, usually a Disney in colour, and of course the very necessary newsreel to serve as a reminder that in your cinematic utopia there was still a war going on outside! There were various information films and food flashes, affording the best possible advice in preparation and use of food, and just how many readers, having spent those war years in the cities, will remember the good old cinema organ and the singalong? I can well see why a night at the pictures was for so many a special occasion.

*"Aid to Russia" Ball in Beverley's Regal Ballroom, from the Beverley Guardian, 27th February 1943.*

*"Wings for Victory Week", through the eyes of the Beverley Guardian, 29th May 1943.*

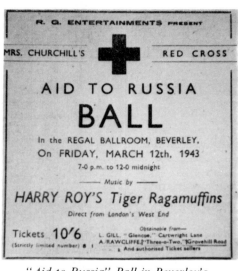

*"Wings for Victory Week", through the eyes of the Beverley Guardian, 29th May 1943.*

*Beverley's "Book Drive" for the Forces, August 1943.*

*Children collecting books, August 1943. Picture reproduced from the "Playhouse News".*

*A different kind of "Explosive", as advertised in the Beverley Guardian, 21st August 1943.*

But what about home entertainment? Well there was the wireless and very popular it was too; in 1940 alone, 9 million licences were issued. Those were the days of the Forces and Home services, "Worker's Playtime", "It's that man again" (or as it was better known ITMA), probably the most popular comedy programme of its day and made so by its anchor-man, Tommy Handley.

The news, especially the 9 o'clock broadcast, was listened to by half the adult population of the country, and for obvious reasons demanded total silence within the household while the more senior members gathered around the wireless to listen, amidst the crackles, to the state of the war.

I wasn't old enough to remember, but I'm sure many readers will recall hearing the familiar voice of Alvar Lidell and the opening words "Here is the news and this is Alvar Lidell reading it..." Those were the years when the

*Collapsed railway bridge, Southcoates Lane, Hull, 14th July 1943. Photo by courtesy of City of Hull Record Office.*

newscasters left behind their anonymity and became national celebrities.

In contrast a good musical output was maintained, and comfort often found in the voices of Gracie Fields and Vera Lynn. However, one voice not welcome but so often found broadcasting on German radio was that of the infamous 'Lord Haw Haw'. This was the name given to William Joyce, an American citizen who was the English Language Propagandist.

A lot of what 'Haw Haw' said was, thankfully, taken lightly by the population, principally due to the German 'expert' scriptwriters whose interpretation and description of events left much to be desired; but even so there was an uncanny closeness to reality. When Joyce became more his own master of the script then his broadcasts would often take a broadside at the British hopes and fears. Although I am unable to confirm it, I'm sure I once heard it said that 'Haw Haw' in one of his broadcasts pinpointed Beverley Minster as a forthcoming target for attack. That so often was the way his output undermined and played on the listener's fears.

From one nasty person to another, a familiar character remembered by many as the rag and bone man. I am told the regular one for Beverley inexplicably disappeared, only to be replaced by a mysterious stranger distinguishable by an enormous ginger beard. He continued in his predecessor's footsteps pushing a pram through the streets of the town, but it has been said he wasn't all he was supposed to be for under his guise many people suspected him of being a spy! One person told of his radio transmitter being concealed in the bottom of the pram and how, when he needed to transmit his information, he went up onto the Westwood, while someone else thought his transmission spot was near Bentley. One point remembered by both who recall this man was that he was eventually captured, but beyond that nothing else is known.

All those cries not to waste water were somewhat 'drowned' one Tuesday afternoon in September when a freak storm arrived over Beverley. The heavens opened and the rain came down, resulting in flooding of the like that had not been seen in the town since 1912. Vast areas were under water; in Lairgate it was a mere six inches.....below window sills! Between Butcher Row and School Lane the water in places was a foot deep; the old Walkergate Beck, dry for some time, was now full, the water bursting through the gratings. In fact very few areas of the town escaped the flooding.

By late September a new water main had been laid bringing with it improved water supplies and at long last allowing all areas of the town a 24 hour supply.

Still with water; way back I mentioned in September 1941 the establishment of static water tanks and how they had been abused by becoming receptacles for all manner of rubbish. In support of this I came across a list of items that had been dumped in these tanks. It made amusing reading, but no doubt posed serious threats to water supplies in an emergency: 26 tea-chests, 1 Anderson shelter, 1 wooden hut, 1 funeral hearse top, 1 complete sofa, 72 milk bottles, 6 rabbit skins and a dead cat! And on top of that, there was a constant fear of the protective fences being broken down and children falling in.

Christmas came again and another year was gone. For many the festive season would once more be a celebration "for the children's sake" only, and a show of brave faces in the numerous family circles that were not complete.

Christmas 1943 was leaner than the last. Shop shelves had less on them and certainly very little in the way of luxuries. However, one could always hope an end to the war was in sight, and who knows, the next Christmas might not be just "for the children's sake".

# 1944

Without question the list of shortages grew almost daily, but that hadn't stopped people making the best of the festive season and the new year, judging from a 'do' organised by the Home Guard members of the Shipyard Platoon. They had a grand night out at the Rambla café where they held a rabbit pie supper and smoking concert. Following the supper, entertainment was provided in the form of monologues, songs and music by an accordionist. The evening was rounded off with everyone singing "Auld Lang Syne" and the National Anthem.

By contrast came the chilling news and certainly the most unwelcome in January, that coal supplies would have to be reduced due to increased demand for the war effort. The south of England could have 4 hundredweight per household while in the north 5 hundredweight was allowed; everyone using coal was urged to start making immediate economies. Tips included using a fire brick in the grate, which could save in the region of $\frac{1}{2}$lb of coal an hour, and keeping the cinders to use the following day. If the room was warm or left unoccupied then it was advisable to bank up with moistened slack (very fine coal, not quite dust), tea leaves or cinders.

The Ministry of Home Security announced a generous offer at the end of January, that for the period up to February 29th (1944 was a leap year) gas masks could be repaired free of charge. Warders would visit properties in their sectors inspecting and replacing any useless ones, but if you had lost your mask then there was no replacement! This campaign formed part of the national effort for everyone to be prepared for any onslaught from the enemy during the coming months.

The popularity of oranges was admirably reflected during early February, with sights of queues for them, and of course the tell-tale orange peel was again littering the streets, reminding one of those good old days of plenty before the war. Fair enough, it was good to have supplies of oranges, but what about an increased supply of batteries for torches, cycle lamps etc. In the coastal towns where a complete blackout was enforced, it was felt that pressure should be brought to bear on the authorities to increase supplies to the area. Towns and cities further inland did have a certain amount of street lighting, but here along the coast there was none.

Do you remember all that trouble over the Weel ferry bridge and its operational hours? Well it was back in the news — the Council was having trouble staffing it. The bridge required manpower of 90 hours a week and attempts had been made repeatedly to find a man, but there was no-one suitable or willing to undertake the job. As an inducement the Council was even prepared to pay 1/- an hour if necessary!

The publication of the Government's white paper outlining the proposed new "free all-in health scheme" raised questions — would it really be free? Some thought it could be part of a scheme to which the public would have to contribute and might cost as much as 4/3 per person per week to fund, which over a year would amount to a substantial sum of money to pay out on top of tax and rates. At this stage it was felt that the idea should be left until after the war, when the scheme could be considered without a political bias.

March brought another reminder from the Ministry of Home Security about the importance of notifying wardens of one's movements and any variations in the number of people living under any roof. Examples were given of the occasion when the Civil Defence spent 48 hours searching for one family who it was later discovered had gone away for the weekend! And another of hours spent digging in a wrecked building only to find the occupants had escaped, but failed to tell the warden. Still with reminders; this time it was to check stirrup pumps. Those left unused could fail when needed in an emergency, so the advice was, test the pump every couple of weeks.

Coalmine strikes and the war situation in April brought cuts in gas and electricity supplies. Although on this occasion domestic supplies were not affected, industry suffered with gas being cut by 25 per cent and electricity by 10 per cent.

"What next?" one asked; reduction in this, scarcity of that. When would it all end — certainly not in the immediate future. From April 17th utility suits were going to cost more, but one tiny consolation came with the abolition of purchase tax on .... go on have a guess .... wooden soled footware!

It's back to water again, and still there was a shortage, this time due to the winter rainfall being only 80 per cent of the average. Although the supply was continuous, economies were still necessary.

Research turns up all manner of interesting facts, as in the case of Carnaby Airfield, for I was to discover that it was not an airfield as such but an emergency runway, or more precisely a 'crash strip'. This was an ideal site, especially being so close to the coast, and it would alleviate the pressure of difficult landings on a nearby operational airfield. Carnaby comprised a single runway running east to west, almost 2 miles long, 700 foot wide and equipped with F.I.D.O. (Fog Investigation and Dispersal Operation). The usefulness of Carnaby is evidenced by the 1,500 landings that took place there during the years 1944 and 1945.

This is probably a good place to mention other airfields in the East Riding, some of which I have to confess I wasn't aware existed. A few miles south of Driffield was Hutton Cranswick serving principally as a transit fighter airfield between January 1942 and July 1945. Cottam was a sort of 'satellite' to Driffield opening in September 1939 and used mainly for bomb storage. Catfoss, originating in the early 1930's, began as a coastal operational training unit on October 1st 1940, and boasted two decoy sites near Dunnington and Skipsea. Then there was Lissett, with the 158 squadron of the RAF arriving in February 1943. Hedon/Hull airfield served as a night landing site, whilst

Brough, besides training the pilots, continued to build aircraft and carry out modifications.

Holme-on-Spalding Moor, or Spaldington as it was locally known, opened in August 1941 under the banner of the No 1 Bomber command.

Operation Overlord was the name given to the invasion of Normandy, the date June 6th 1944, D-Day. This was the second front destined to attack German troops in Europe's mainland. For quite some time preparations had been going on in secret for the invasion. Even day trips to the south coast were banned, keeping from prying eyes the vast quantities of military equipment concealed within the Hampshire countryside in readiness for that vital day. Along the east coast dummy tanks and landing craft were parked in an attempt to fool enemy reconnaissance planes. I have also heard it said that telegraph poles were positioned, painted and pointed towards Europe to give the enemy the impression that a battery of guns was in readiness.

To help the landing of the Allied troops, enormous floating concrete platforms over 180 feet long were built and stored ready to be towed across the channel. And PLUTO, that ingenious pipeline under the sea, was also ready to supply oil to the armies after they had landed.

As the battle commenced the troops, American, British and Canadian, began the task of loosening the Nazi grip on Europe. Within a week of their successful landing, revenge attacks were being launched by Germany and 'V-1's were speeding towards our coasts and London in particular (the 'V' standing for *Vergeltungswaffe* or 'reprisal weapon'). These pilotless, flying bombs, better known as 'doodlebugs' or 'buzz bombs', were the enemy, and lethal. In brief the flying bomb comprised a warhead loaded with high explosives, a fuel tank, guidance controls and a propulsion unit. These bombs arrived overhead at high speed, causing tension to rise as the sinister engine note ceased and the bomb silently plummeted to earth. People knew that when the fuel ran out and the engine cut they had fifteen seconds of fear-ridden helplessness in which they could hope and pray that it would not fall on them. Later in the year the 'V-1' was superseded by the 'V-2' which carried more explosives and arrived silently with no warning, heralded only by the actual explosion. Temporary relief from these bombs came when the Allied advances captured some of the 'V-1' launching sites.

Remember earlier the note about the dogs being 'called-up'; well one Beverley dog had his 'call-up' papers. The black alsatian labrador belonging to Mr A.S. Marson, butcher of Walkergate, left the town for training at the Ministry of Aircraft Production Guard Dog Training School where his role, when trained, was to guard aircraft and the like from possible sabotage.

It was 'that' time of year again and the call was out to support the war effort investing in savings bonds. 1944 brought 'Salute the Soldier' and the target figure was set at £300,000. As in previous years the week offered a full programme of events, although the entertainment was repetitious of earlier war efforts. The opening ceremony was heralded by the Band of the East Yorkshire

MINISTRY OF FUEL AND POWER ANNOUNCEMENT

# COAL SUPPLIES
## DURING MAY AND JUNE

Supplies to domestic and other controlled premises are subject to the following restrictions during the period 1st May—30th June:—

1. **HOUSE and KITCHEN COAL and "COALITE"**

   No controlled premises may be supplied with more than 15 cwt. in the aggregate of fuels in this group during the period 1st May—30th June.

   **THIS IS THE MAXIMUM, NOT A RATION. IN SOME DISTRICTS SUPPLIES WILL NOT BE AVAILABLE TO PROVIDE THE MAXIMUM QUANTITY FOR CONSUMERS. PREFERENCE WILL BE GIVEN TO CONSUMERS WHO ARE WITHOUT STOCKS AND WHO ARE ENTIRELY DEPENDENT ON COAL**

   No delivery of these fuels may be made to any premises where the total stock exceeds 30 cwt., or which would raise the stock above 30 cwt.

2. **SMALL ANTHRACITE and WELSH DRY STEAM COAL, COKE (other than coke breeze) and MANUFACTURED FUELS (other than "Coalite")**

   Fuels in this group may be obtained, if available, up to an aggregate maximum of one ton during the period 1st May—30th June provided that no consumer obtains any supply if his stock exceeds two tons or which would raise his stock above two tons. **(There is no restriction on large Anthracite or Coke Breeze).**

   The time has not yet come for building up your full winter's stock. You can make a start by buying what you can within the limits set out above, and exercising the greatest possible economy in the use of all forms of fuel.

   No carry over is permitted of quantities which have not been obtained in previous restriction periods.

**Issued by the Local Fuel Overseer for the BEVERLEY BOROUGH AND RURAL DISTRICT, Municipal Offices, Lairgate, Beverley**

## We must SAVE FUEL for Battle

*"Save Fuel" Campaign, in the Beverley Guardian, 13th May 1944.*

# Action pictures!

The Army Film and Photographic Unit urgently need cameras to provide pictures of troops and equipment in action during the coming offensive. Four makes of camera are specially required:

LEICA
SUPER IKONTA
CONTAX
ROLLEIFLEX

Anyone owning one of these cameras now has the chance of sending it into battle to take pictures which will be part of history! The need is urgent!

## What do I do . . . ?

If I own a camera in good working order, of any of the makes above, I send full details of it at once to the Ministry of Supply, I.P. 7c, 1 Charing Cross, London, S.W.1. I do *not* send the camera itself until I receive an official offer to purchase.

*Issued by the Ministry of Information*

**Space presented to the Nation by the Brewers' Society**

*Appeal for cameras, 17th June 1944.*

# WOT! NO STAFF?

Exactly, Mr. Chad. Some serving man is likely to go short of refreshment and relaxation because Naafi is short of staff. To maintain its canteen service at full efficiency, Naafi must have —and have quickly—the assistance of many more women who are willing to work in canteens. *You* can help, particularly if you have worked in a shop or can cook a simple meal. With this knowledge and experience you are well qualified to

## TAKE A PAID JOB WITH NAAFI

Naafi needs for service at Home many more canteen manageresses, counter assistants and women with knowledge of home cooking to train as cooks. (Opportunities for service overseas after period of training in Home establishments.) Write *now* for details of pay, conditions of service, etc., to Staff Manager :

**NAAFI (Dept.     ) MUSEUM CHAMBERS, MUSEUM STREET, YORK.**

THE OFFICIAL CANTEEN ORGANISATION FOR H.M. FORCES IN WAR AND IN PEACE

*Remember the "Chads"? The NAAFI needs women in 1944!*

# PRISONERS OF WAR
## (NEXT-OF-KIN)

●

During the Winter months, and commencing the 12th October, the offices of the above at 36, Market Place, will be open from 7 p.m. to 8-30 p.m., instead of 9 p.m., when the Committee will be pleased to help all next-of-kin with their problems

*Help for the families of Prisoners of War, 7th October 1944.*

*"Salute The Soldier Week", June 1944. Frame enlargement from film taken by Ernest Symmons. Note the dome-topped buses specially built to get through Beverley's North Bar.*

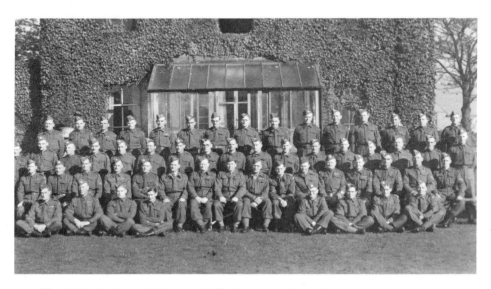

*The No.5 Molescroft Platoon, "E" Company, the 3rd East Riding (Beverley) Battalion Home Guard, 1st October 1944.*

Regiment at the Market Cross, and on the Sunday there was the Civic Parade. Each day of the week was earmarked as a Special Day — Civic, Ladies, Industries, Tradesmen, Rural and Farmers — Saturday ending the week with Groups and Children's Day. There were dances at the Regal Ballroom with music provided by the bands of the East Yorkshire Regiment and Tommy Fisher. Whoever's band you chose to dance to the tickets were only 5/- and if those legs yearned to go on dancing then for 1/- there was outdoor dancing. However, you didn't have to participate — as alternatives for those who tired watching other people get tired, there were various exhibitions and displays to attract, entertain and instruct including a demonstration in the Market Place of Anti-Aircraft guns.

Once again the week was a success, realising a total of £331,427 which brought the total raised through savings over the four years of these special weeks to £1,300,480. This represented an average of £325,120 for each effort.

An attempt on Hitler's life came on July 20th when some of his own colonels tried to assassinate him. Hitler escaped death, but it seems certain that this contributed to a further deterioration in his already failing health.

Are you old enough to remember, or have you heard about, the Carnival Queen contests held in Beverley and so much a feature of town life before the war? Well I was pleased to discover the war didn't allow the local "talent" to be totally ignored or forgotten thanks to the Armstrongs Patents' Sports and Social Association, who organised a 'Munition Queen' contest. The judging took place at a dance in Armstrong's clubroom. For the two hundred people present the atmosphere was tense, and the decision was difficult, but eventually Miss Marie Wilson was declared the winner, with Miss M. Helyland, Miss J. Marin and Miss M. Twiddy as runners up. The lucky "Queen" was presented with a cheque for five pounds by Mr Harry Popple, Manager of the Marble Arch Cinema, and the runners up were not forgotten, each receiving a cheque for one pound.

The first official duty for the winning lady was on July 23rd when the 'Munition Queen' opened the Grand Gymkhana on the Norwood cricket ground. The event was organised by Armstrong's Social Group, and was in place of their annual day's outing, which as a result of restricted travel regulations was cancelled.

(Most of the major industries in the town organised an annual day trip to somewhere. I remember as a child going on the Hodgson's Tannery one, which I recall took the company's employees and their families on a day trip to Scarborough. These outings were pleasant, but I always enjoyed the train journey the most.)

On September 8th the first 'V-2' rocket fell on England.

If it should happen that your "stay at home" was dull, boring and without excitement, then a fair amount of time could be passed at the Regal Cinema, who were screening the epic "Gone with the Wind". That, thanks to its length, would effectively take up half a day.

Still at the pictures, this time the Playhouse and a Royal visitor to the matinee. Her Royal Highness the Princess Royal, whilst visiting W.V.S. centres in the area, was invited to the Playhouse to see the film made by Mr Ernest Symmons, of the work done by W.V.S. Hospital Helps and their contributions to the Emergency Hospital, along with a film of the Princess's visit in 1941. This was the first time in the cinema's history that a Royal visitor had been to the Playhouse, although of course many had appeared on its screen, and this was indeed an honour. The Princess Royal arrived and was greeted by a Guard of Honour of Hospital Helps at the entrance to the cinema. Once she was inside the audience quickly recognised the Princess and gave her a real 'Yorkshire Welcome'.

Showing around this time was a film with a title I'm sure many wished was true, "The Strange Death of Hitler", but no, this film was only based on a best seller.

With the Autumn nights drawing into Winter, and for the first time since the war began, evening services left the Playhouse and returned to St Mary's Church. In many respects there was an easing in restrictions as now the blackout had become more of a 'dim out' — the tide of war had well and truly turned. Talk was now of post-war housing and those well respected homes the 'prefabs'.

Many felt a sadness as the comradeship the war had generated began to fade. This was the time for disbandment and standing down of the Home Guard, the wardens and the like. In fact the Playhouse news showed the film of the Home Guard's last parade on November 12th 1944. At least the film record would for some time in the future stir the memory to remind everyone of their efforts.

December 24th and the arrival of an early and unwanted Christmas present in the unpleasant shape of a flying bomb, destined for industrial sites over in West Yorkshire and Lancashire. This one fell on the outskirts of Hull, landing in a field. Even so the damage it caused was extensive with repair work to some properties taking over six months to complete.

Another year had passed, it seemed to go even faster than the last, but then are another year older and the older you get the faster the years seem to go! This Christmas would again host a good many empty chairs around the Christmas table, but even with traditional fare being only marginally better than last year, at least an end to the war was felt to be in sight. Still the question was asked — is Hitler dead, or alive and insane? Some actually believed he was now mad and no longer in charge of operations, others thought him dead.

# 1945

Not a good start to the New Year with news that on January 1st Germany had launched an offensive, known as Operation Norwind, against the United States Seventh Army.

The weather was very seasonal, heavy snow having fallen over a number of days making walking and riding very difficult. Snow ploughs made their mark in keeping many of the town's roads clear, but the youngsters wished the snow to last for a long time as they, and many adults, were enjoying some of the best toboganning for many years, Hill 60 on the Westwood proving by far the most popular place to be. But as the thaw came so did the burst pipes, and with the shortage of labour plumbers worked round the clock to meet the demand made upon them.

Once again the Playhouse Cinema hosted the underprivileged. On this occasion about 70 evacuee children, including some who had been in Beverley for over five years, were entertained at the pictures and then for tea at the Rambla cafe where each child was given 1/- and a packet of sweets.

On February 13th RAF bombers raided Dresden. The following day, aircraft of the United States Eighth Air Force also bombed Dresden, and Budapest fell to the Red Army.

Sunday March 4th and another raid, this time with cannon shells and machine guns. This affected a wide area of the East Riding but thankfully no injuries were reported and damage was not serious.

March 7th and the announcement that our troops and those of the 9th Armoured Division had crossed the Rhine at Remagen. Two days later on the 9th, American 'B-29's commenced incendiary campaigns against major Japanese cities.

Back in Hull, what was to be the city's last raid of the war took place on the 17th and 18th of March, affecting a great number of domestic properties in Holderness Road, Morrill Street and Holland Street. Although the outcome of this attack was recorded as "little damage", 12 people lost their lives and 22 were seriously injured.

In a surprise move on March 22nd, the Rhine at Oppenheim was crossed by troops of America's Third Army. The following day, the 23rd, the British Second Army crossed the Rhine near Rees.·
March 27th saw the end of attacks by the feared 'V-2' rocket. This date was the last on which bombs fell on England.

Not a day for fools, April 1st saw the capture of Okinawa by U.S. troops, whilst April 7th said goodbye to the Japanese Superbattleship 'Yamato' when it was sunk. Back in Europe the 13th was unlucky for some, when Vienna fell to the Soviet Army. On the 23rd Himmler made a surrender offer to the Western Allies.

April 25th brought together American and Soviet forces near Torgau effectively breaking Germany in two. Three days later, on the 28th Mussolini and his mistress, Clara Petacci, were executed by partisans.

On April 29th, Adolf Hitler married his mistress, Eva Braun, and the following day they committed suicide. The Führer had not only destroyed himself but had in effect destroyed 'his' Germany and 'his' people. (Some still firmly believe Hitler's death was in fact faked and that he secretly escaped —one of the war's unsolved mysteries).

May 2nd and the Soviet Army completed its capture of Berlin, while in Italy German Forces surrendered. On the 5th surrender came from German Forces in the Netherlands, North Western Germany and Denmark. In Bavaria the fighting ended for the G Group of the German Army.

Finally in the early hours of May 7th 1945 the war against Germany ended with all their Forces unconditionally surrendering.

The day following was one to linger in the memory of many for a great number of years. V.E. Day had at last arrived. 'Victory in Europe' was indeed cause for celebration, but the war hadn't completely ended; that wouldn't be for a few more months yet as there was still the war with Japan to contend with.


But here and now the war with Germany was over. This was the time to sound church bells, light bonfires and dance in the streets. Services were held in the churches everywhere remembering the many that would never return and thanking God for peace at last. Throughout the country processions representing the Army, Navy and Air Force, marched through town and city alike to streets lined with crowds who warmly applauded the respective services as they passed. This picture was not just local, but was reflected throughout the land.

Here in Beverley the V.E. celebrations were no exception; street parties abounded with "sumptuous" tea parties, fireworks and bonfires. The Holme Church Lane bonfire had an effigy of Hitler hanging in the centre and as the fire burned, so a great many of the local populace danced around until it was little more than a pile of ashes; but the ashes of war were throughout the country in abundance, and the scars would take years to heal. And of the people, so many lives had been lost, and so very many people crippled both physically and mentally — sadly for them the war would never end.

Now there was hope on the horizon for a new and better Britain, but it would take time, patience and money to build on that new day that had just dawned.

Happier days had already arrived as numerous prisoners of war started to come home. Their welcome was tumultuous, with tearful reunions. In the words of Sgt. Stanley Kent-Payne "Our reception was marvellous. It was overwhelming and to think that one day we were in Germany and the next at home."

And 'back at home' on Sunday May 27th around 100 repatriated prisoners of war, along with parents and friends, went for tea at the Rambla cafe by invitation of the owner.

After tea it was off to the Marble Arch Cinema for the Victory Concert where entertainment was provided with a variety of music that was enjoyed and appreciated by a capacity audience.

And still the V.E. celebrations continued. There could not have been many, if any, parts of the town that had not in some way been actively involved in a celebration of some sort. The Albert Terrace victory party was funded from a penny-a-week subscription from residents and fire-watchers. Originally this money had been intended to support those who had suffered bomb damage, but thankfully the money wasn't required for this purpose and it was decided the children should benefit. The party started with tea in the Drill Hall (now the Doctors surgery), Rambla cafe doing the honours, and after everyone had had their fill the presentation of a five pound note was made to Corporal Morris of the Green Howards who had been repatriated after the capitulation of Germany. As if the children hadn't had enough to eat, it was ice cream and soft drinks all round, then out to the playing fields for the sports (and on full stomachs!). Later it was back to the Drill Hall for games and community singing, but when darkness fell another surprise awaited, a spectacular firework display. All too soon the party was over but there was still one last treat in store, for each child was given 5 shillings upon leaving for home.

Do you remember, readers, earlier about the Pale Moon Coffee Stall that Mr Gordon Armstrong so kindly established in the Market Place during the first winter of the war? Its services had almost come to an end, but through black-outs and all weathers the stall had provided an estimated quarter of a million cups of tea and coffee not just to Forces members but to the unfortunate people of Hull who had left the city during the raids and had no means of obtaining hot drinks during the severe blitzes on Hull. Mr Armstrong personally opened the stall at six each morning and kept it open until everyone had been served, opening again at six in the evening right through until midnight.

Following closely on the heels of the victory celebrations came the debate on the future of the coalition government that had operated throughout the war. Churchill wanted it to continue until the surrender of Japan, but Clement Atlee had different ideas. He was leader of the Labour Party and preferred an early General Election. So, on July 5th the first election for ten years was held, but this was no easy election as many voters were service personnel still overseas, and of course there were a great number of the population who had changed addresses. However 73% of the electorate voted, which came as a considerable surprise to many, but the results wouldn't be known until the postal votes had been counted.

The Potsdam Conference on July 17th brought both Churchill and Atlee together, and in reviewing a victory parade in Berlin it was noticed that Atlee was cheered by the British Soldiers at least as much, if not more, than Churchill, causing some to question the result of the vote.

*Waste paper makes plaster board.
Advertisement from Beverley
Guardian, April 1945.*

*Utility furniture, October
1945.*

*Coal entitlement, October 1945.*

*V.E. Celebrations, outside the Fulford Dance Hall, Beverley Road, Hull, May
1945. Photos by courtesy of Kath Finch.*

The nail-biting wait was over, for on July 26th the Conservatives were defeated and Churchill resigned. The election had brought a landslide victory for Labour, with Atlee as the new Prime Minister. The result was still a puzzle to many — how could Churchill have failed, he who had led the country through six years of war and its 'finest hour'? But for the six years ahead Atlee would do battle on a different front in a fight to bring the country back to a level of economic recovery.

August 6th, and a day for the history books. Hiroshima became the first victim of the Atomic bomb. Two days later on the 8th, Russia declared war on Japan. The following day it was the turn of the city of Nagasaki to receive the Atomic bomb.

Although it had been expected, it wasn't until August 14th that Japan surrendered, bringing the war to an end when they finally signed the instrument of surrender on September 2nd 1945.

The war was at long last over and in celebration of the victory over Japan, parties and activities on similar lines to the V.E. celebrations were in full swing, many children hardly able to believe their luck at having two parties in a matter of months! Once again their little stomachs were filled with cakes, ice cream and pop while the adults danced the night away.

Work had now started on two new housing sites, one at Walkington, the other at Newbald, with the initial preparation of streets, sewers and water mains being carried out by German Prisoners of War who were employed by the contractors. They were paid the full union rate, but only received a maximum of 3/- per week, or as a tradesman 6/-. The difference between what the P.O.W.s were paid and received was taken for food, accommodation and transportation.

September 15th brought the opening of national Thanksgiving Week with a target set for Beverley and District of £250,000. Like previous years when these special weeks were held the recipe was as before, with dancing, social events, concerts and a late night matinee at the cinema. The pattern was repeated and the target was once again exceeded, reaching £331,427.

In September 1945 one of the first temporary bungalows was completed in Beverley's Watts Road, the council offering anyone the opportunity to inspect, but admission was by ticket! We knew those temporary houses as prefabs. This was the name given to those millions of prefabricated homes that sprang up throughout the country. We lived in Beverley's Goths Lane and even though prefabs were only supposed to be homes for about ten years, ours served us well for just over twenty years. And it wasn't too bad either with two decent sized bedrooms, a living room, entrance hall, bathroom with separate loo, and kitchen complete with folding table, gas fridge, and cooker. It was a sad day for my parents when we left that "temporary bungalow" as it had been their first home after the war.

Do you recall reading earlier about the fund raising for the safe removal and storage of the Beverley Minster's east window? Well, the window had been safely stored in the Percy Chapel and in the Autumn of 1945 was replaced.

*Special Constables (War-time) and Air Raid Wardens, based at Hodgson's Tannery, Beverley.*

The Remembrance or Armistice Day on November 11th 1945 was the day to see tears in the eyes of those remembering their loved ones who had been killed in both the First and Second World Wars. This day would, like the anniversaries in each family's life, live in and sting the hearts of so many for a great number of years ahead, and in some cases for a lifetime.

Christmas was sneaking up again, and this one just had to be better than those in previous years now there was no war. But so many of those long awaited Christmas luxuries were still a long way off and shortages, along with rationing, would continue for a good many years ahead. Thankfully, though, the Christmas of 1945 could reflect the Christmas carol words "Peace on earth", and as this festive season came and went it was a time for remembering those Christmasses past — the ones ahead could only get better and it was hoped that all those days between each Christmas would too.

As I sit writing this in 1989 I cast my mind back to what I could remember, not from the war years, but of those monuments to war that lingered around for so many years after hostilities had ended. The air raid shelters - I can remember one at Spencer School and in Dyer Lane. I recall as a child exploring and playing in one of those search light and 'ak ak' gun emplacements on the land south of Hull Bridge Road, and that's about it, with the exception of the Emergency Hospital and its wooden-hutted wards — which is still there in 1989 as the Westwood Hospital. Then of course the monument to both wars this century, the cenotaph, not just here in our town, but every town, city and great many villages throughout the county, a lasting symbol to the memory of those who gave to save. We should remember them with thanks always.

*"Be Prepared" – The Home Guard's kit.*

# BIBLIOGRAPHY

Campbell, Christy      "The World War II Fact Book 1939-1945"
(Futura 1986).

Chamberlain, E.R.,      "Life in Wartime Britain"
English Life Series
(B.T. Batsford Ltd. 1972).

Geraghty, T.,      "A North-East Coast Town: Ordeal and
Triumph"
(A. Brown & Sons Ltd. 1951).

Gilmour, Ian,      "Britain at War 1939-45"
Exploring History Series
(Oliver & Boyd 1982).

Halpenny, Bruce Barrymore      "Action Stations"
(Patrick Stephens Ltd. 1982).

Kelsall, Freda,      "How We Used To Live 1936-1953"
(Macdonald with Yorkshire Television 1981).

Lewis, Peter,      "A People's War"
(Thames Methuen & Channel Four 1986).

Ramsey, Winston G.,      "The Blitz Then and Now, Vol 1"
(After the Battle Magazine 1987).

Rapier, Brian J.,      "White Rose Base"
(Air Museum, York Publications 1980).

Robinson, Peter Harvatt,      "The Home of Beautiful Pictures"
(Hutton Press 1985).

Seaman, L.C.B.,      "Life in Britain Between the Wars"
English Life Series
(B.T. Batsford 1970).

Beverley Guardians 1938 to 1945
(East Yorkshire Newspapers Ltd.)